MW00873179

# NO SUGAR,
# NO FLOUR,
# NO FUSS!

## Soveya's
## Incredibly Easy & Healthy
## Cookbook

300 Recipes – Great for Diabetics and Gluten-Free Diets

Eli Glaser, Editor

Zakah Glaser, Editor

Eleventh Edition        ©Soveya 2020 All rights reserved.

## DISCLAIMER

# Table of Contents

# EATING TO SATISFACTION IS THE GREATEST BLESSING
# soveya
so · VEY · ah

Soveya is a Hebrew word meaning **satisfied**. It's often found in the Torah (the Jewish Bible) as well as Talmudic teachings in the context of eating.

One of the primary sources is in the book of Deuteronomy (*Devarim*), chapter 8, verse 10: *"And you will eat, and you will be satisfied, and you will bless the Lord."*

The fundamental values we derive from this verse can inform and enrich our relationship with food. And as you'll see, this is why I chose the name Soveya.

I'll focus on three words in the sentence: to *eat*; to be *satisfied*; and to *bless*.

To *eat*. The purpose of eating is to provide our bodies with the essential nutrients we need to survive. Take away our food, and we will die. It's that simple. Therefore, eating - by definition - should be an act that brings health, vitality, and life to a person.

If we engage in acts of eating that run contrary to that goal - we are causing ourselves harm instead of health and are not fulfilling the function of food for which it was intended. As the classic scholar Maimonides wrote more than 1,000 years ago: *"Overeating is like poison for anyone and it is the primary cause of all illness. Most illnesses are caused either by eating harmful foods or overeating even healthy foods."* (Laws of Knowledge, chapter 4, paragraph 15).

To be **satisfied**: We are directed to eat in order to satisfy our body's need for nutrition and sustenance - to provide us the energy and well-being to carry out our purpose in this world. As we have all experienced, eating beyond this point is an easy and alluring trap into which to fall. Food is tempting and tastes good; it provides comfort, convenience and an emotional elixir for stress and anxiety. It might make us momentarily merry, but we're often left much less than happy. Filling our stomach isn't necessarily fulfilling. Stuffed isn't satisfied.

To **bless**: If we're able to maintain our boundaries, make the right choices and eat the right amounts, we're left feeling extremely grateful, content and satisfied. The fact that the food was flavorsome, appetizing and a physically enjoyable experience adds greatly to our gratification.

We're commanded to capture that moment and use it as a springboard for appreciation – to recognize that food is an incredibly special and vital gift for us to preserve our health and to acknowledge the source from where it originated.

Connecting these three ideas certainly helps concretize the concept that eating to satisfaction is truly one of the greatest blessings.

## ABOUT THIS COOKBOOK

The recipes included in this cookbook are very easy and simple and do not include any sugar, added sweeteners, or flour. Neither do they include any obscure or unusual ingredients. Most recipes should not take much time to prepare.

This cookbook is for people who would ideally like to eat healthier food, but are daunted by the prospect of extensive or complicated food preparation. If you don't enjoy spending hours in the kitchen, or simply don't know much about how to cook healthy items— then this cookbook is for you.

### FOR THOSE WHO FOLLOW A SPECIALIZED FOOD PLAN

There is a section at the end of the cookbook entitled "Single Serving Dishes". The amounts given for each recipe may differ from your particular food plan and will need to be adjusted accordingly.

The remaining recipes are primarily for families. However, many of them can be easily adapted for individuals who weigh and measure their meals according to food plans with specific guidelines. You can do it in one of two ways:

(A) Prepare all the ingredients together as called for in the recipe and then weigh your specific portions separately before eating.
(B) Cook each food group individually, weigh them and then mix together before eating.

The instructions for many of the recipes call for sautéing the ingredients, without specifying whether to use oil or not. It is up to your discretion to sauté using oil or by simply spraying a pan with non-stick spray.

## SUCCESSFUL WEIGHT LOSS IS NOT ABOUT LOSING WEIGHT!

It's not about ketosis, calculating calories, or counting points. It's about the courage to step outside your comfort zone and get off the dieting rollercoaster. Enough is finally enough.

If you really want to meet your goal to actually maintain a healthy body size, then you must stop focusing on changing your weight and start focusing on changing yourself and your relationship with food. That's the underlying message of the Soveya Solution.

The Soveya Solution is a proven and practical system developed by Eli Glaser after his struggles with morbid obesity and the life-changing turnaround 17 years ago that enabled him to shed 130 pounds – and keep it off! Eli has mastered a unique, highly effective approach to weight loss and lifestyle change and walks you step-by-step through this transformative process, providing innovative and pragmatic tools along with clear and concrete guidelines – all positioned atop a platform infused with positivity, humor and endless encouragement.

Eli's vulnerability and raw honesty lend a richness and relatability that penetrates the heart of all who have shared the battle of the bulge. This groundbreaking system has impacted thousands of people around the world. It's not just a weight changer and it's not even a game changer. It's a life changer.

For more information about any of Soveya's services or to order more cookbooks, visit our website or contact us at:

1-888-8-SOVEYA (876-8392)
info@soveya.com
www.soveya.com

# DEDICATIONS

In honor of Dorothy Hinde, and in loving memory of Jack Hinde, Sidney Glaser and Sarah Glaser, our incredible loving parents who have been supportive of us in every way imaginable. May their unconditional love, encouragement, assistance, and sponsorship of our efforts be a tremendous merit for them.

## IN GRATITUDE

I owe a huge debt of gratitude to our dedicated volunteers, Nechama Rotshtein, Molly Cypkin, Deena Perelmuter, and Dorothy Hinde for their tireless work and devotion to make this cookbook a reality. A big thank you to all the people who contributed recipes. Much thanks to Adina Michelson for your invaluable guidance.

Thank you to Frank and Danielle Sarah Storch and family for helping to sponsor the publication of this cookbook.

My boundless appreciation goes to my extraordinary husband, Eli Glaser, and our fabulous children for your support, patience, and enthusiasm in helping me bring this project to fruition.

My eternal gratitude to the Almighty for helping me break free from the shackles of food addiction and allowing me to utilize my experiences to help others.

Zakah Glaser, Editor

# NUTRITION 101 – THE SIX ESSENTIAL NUTRIENTS

Nutrients are chemical substances found in the foods we eat and are needed for the body to develop and function properly. There are six essential nutrients:

## CARBOHYDRATES (CARBS)

Carbs give quick energy and hold stored energy. There are, however, healthy carbs as well as carbs that are bad for the body. Healthy carbs, such as fruits and vegetables and brown rice, stabilize blood-sugar levels. Most refined and processed carbs such as cookies, crackers, white bread, and white rice, are rapidly metabolized, causing a spike in blood sugar levels, and result in hunger soon after eating. This causes cravings for more food.

## PROTEINS

Proteins help the body repair itself, build muscle and bone, and give energy. Standard proteins are meat, poultry, fish, dairy, legumes, and eggs. Healthy proteins make the body feel satisfied.

## FATS

Fats give energy, keep the body warm, and maintain healthy skin. The body uses whatever fat it needs for energy, and the rest is stored in the body's fat cells. Unsaturated fats, such as nuts and olive oil, are healthy.

## VITAMINS

Vitamins are necessary for normal body functions, mental alertness, and resistance to infection. Certain vitamins help produce blood cells and hormones in your nervous system. Eating a balanced diet, including lots of fruits and vegetables, is the best way to get the vitamins the body needs.

## MINERALS

Minerals help the body grow, make strong bones and teeth, and keep blood healthy. Major minerals include calcium, phosphorus, and magnesium. Sodium, potassium and chloride, known as electrolytes, are important in regulating water and chemical balance in your body.

## WATER

Water keeps body temperature regulated and flushes waste products from your body. Water keeps your body organs functioning, your brain sharp, and your skin clear.

# Breakfast

# &

# Dairy

## OATMEAL PANCAKES

1 C. fruit (blueberries, strawberries, bananas, apples)
1 C. Old-Fashioned oats

4 eggs
2 T. nuts (optional)

Put all the ingredients into a blender and process until smooth. Spray a nonstick pan and preheat over medium heat. Pour half of the mixture into the pan and cook for 4-5 minutes. Flip the pancake and cook until the inside is cooked. Repeat with remaining batter.

## OVERNIGHT OATMEAL

1 C. milk
1/4 C. dry milk
1 C. Old-Fashioned oats
14 dried apricot halves, diced

1 dried fig, diced
2 T. golden raisins
4 C. water

Whip the milk and dry milk in a blender. Mix with remaining ingredients, transfer to a crock pot and set to low heat. Cover and cook overnight. If you don't have a dairy crock pot, heat gently in a regular pot until it comes to a slow boil, simmer until desired consistency.

## OATMEAL DELIGHT

2 eggs
1/2 C. cottage cheese

1/4 C. Old-Fashioned oats
1/8 tsp. salt

Mix ingredients well. Drop by tablespoons onto hot pan or griddle that has been sprayed with vegetable spray. Turn over when bubbles appear on surface and cook 1 more minute. Serve with fresh berries or fruit.

# BAKED OATMEAL WITH APPLE

2 C. milk or unsweetened soy
  milk
1 T. ground cinnamon
1 C. egg whites or 8 eggs

4 C. uncooked Old-Fashioned
  oats
2 C. apples, peeled and diced

Preheat oven to 350°F. In a large bowl, combine milk and cinnamon. In another bowl, beat egg whites or eggs, and then mix with milk mixture. Add oatmeal and mix well. Fold in apples and pour into greased baking dish. Bake 40-50 minutes. Serves 8.

# HEARTY QUINOA BREAKFAST

1 C. cooked quinoa
1 apple, diced
1/2 C. plain yogurt, or more as
  needed

Handful chopped walnuts or
almonds

Combine all the ingredients. Substitute other fruits or nuts of your choice, if desired.

# QUINOA CEREAL

1/2 C. quinoa
1 C. water or milk

1 C. crushed pineapple, drained
1/2 tsp. cinnamon

Bring water or milk to a boil, add quinoa and simmer covered until water is absorbed, about 10 minutes. Fold in pineapple and serve.

# FRUITED QUINOA BREAKFAST

1/2 C. dry quinoa, well-rinsed
1 1/2 C. milk or unsweetened soy
  milk

2 T. raisins
1 C. apricots, chopped
1/4 tsp. vanilla extract*

Combine quinoa and milk in a medium saucepan. Bring to boil, then lower heat and simmer covered for about 10-15 minutes, until the quinoa is tender. Stir in raisins, apricots, and vanilla. Cook an additional 2 minutes. Serve warm or chilled.
*Vanilla extract contains sweeteners and should be omitted by those refraining from sweeteners.

## QUICK & EASY BREAKFAST SOUFFLÉ

4 egg whites, slightly beaten         1/2 C. applesauce
1/2 C. Old-Fashioned oats

Spray bowl with nonstick spray. Place all ingredients in bowl, mix well and microwave, covered, for 2 minutes.

## SALSA OMELET

4 whole eggs                    1/2 C. cheddar cheese,
6 egg whites                       shredded
3/4 C. salsa                    4 T. sour cream

Whisk together eggs and egg whites. Pour eggs into greased frying pan. When top sets, spoon salsa on half of the eggs and sprinkle with cheese. Fold the other half of the omelet over salsa and cheese. Slip onto a plate and divide into servings. Spoon sour cream over top of each serving.

## DEVILED EGGS

6 hard boiled eggs, peeled and      1/2 tsp. white vinegar
   cut lengthwise                   1/8 tsp. salt
1/4 C. mayonnaise                   1/4 tsp. black pepper
1/2 tsp. dry ground mustard         Paprika for garnish

Remove the egg yolks to a small bowl and mash with a fork. Add mayonnaise, mustard powder, vinegar, salt and pepper and mix thoroughly. Fill the empty egg white shells with the mixture and sprinkle lightly with paprika.

# ONION CREPES

**Crepe:**
6 eggs
2 T. olive oil
Salt

**Filling:**
2 sweet Vidalia onions, diced
1/8 tsp. salt
1/8 tsp. black pepper
Dash of paprika

These egg crepes are more like a very thin omelet than a crepe. Beat the eggs, oil and salt together. Heat a greased small pan over medium heat until hot. Place 2 tablespoons of egg mixture into pan. Cook until the bottom is browned. Carefully flip over and cook about one more minute. Slide crepe onto a plate. Continue making crepes until egg mixture is gone.

Sauté onions and spices until golden brown. Place onion mixture (use a liberal amount but not too much so that it doesn't spill out of the crepe) about a quarter of the way in on one side of the blintz. Roll the crepe over the filling, keeping it tight. Your filling will fall out if you've rolled the crepe loosely. Place the filled crepe seam side down on the plate so it doesn't open.

# SPINACH RICOTTA OMELET

3 eggs
3 egg whites
1 C. ricotta cheese
10 oz. frozen chopped spinach
   or 1 C. fresh baby spinach

1/4 tsp. ground nutmeg
1/4 C. Parmesan cheese
1/4 tsp. salt
1/4 tsp. black pepper

Mix ricotta, spinach, nutmeg, salt, pepper and Parmesan cheese in a bowl. Beat eggs and egg whites. Fold ricotta-spinach mixture into eggs. Spray a large frying pan with nonstick spray, add egg mixture and cook over medium heat without stirring. Cook until mixture starts to brown on the sides. Fold in half carefully and then try to gently flip to other side.

# LOX FRITTATA

| | |
|---|---|
| 1/4 medium onion, chopped | 6 eggs |
| Salt and pepper to taste | 2 T. milk |
| 4 oz. smoked salmon | 2 T. plain yogurt |
| 8 black olives, chopped | 8 oz. cream cheese, cubed |

Preheat the oven to 350° F. Sauté onion, salt and pepper until translucent. Add the salmon and olives; cook and stir briefly. In a medium bowl, whisk together the eggs, milk and yogurt. Stir in salmon and onion. Pour mixture into greased baking pan and scatter cubes of cream cheese over the top. Bake for 20 minutes, or until browned. Flip onto a serving plate, and cut into wedges to serve.

# PARMESAN FRITTATA

| | |
|---|---|
| 1 onion, thinly sliced | 1/3 C. grated Parmesan cheese |
| 5 eggs | 1/4 tsp. salt |
| 4 egg whites | 1 medium tomato, thinly sliced |
| black pepper to taste | 1 tsp. dried basil |

Sauté onion until golden. Remove from heat.
Place eggs and egg whites in a blender with salt, pepper and Parmesan cheese. Blend until smooth. Stir egg mixture with onions. Place in a greased baking pan. Arrange tomatoes and basil over the top. Broil in oven until browned. Cut into wedges and serve.

# COTTAGE CHEESE LOAF

| | |
|---|---|
| 1 qt. cottage cheese | 3 T. onion flakes |
| 1 C. chopped nuts | 1 T. salt |
| 5 eggs, beaten | 1 C. water |
| 1/4 C. melted butter | |

Combine all ingredients together and bake in a greased casserole dish for 1 hour at 350°F.

## SPINACH, CHEESE AND TOMATO BAKE

1/2 C. cottage cheese
1/2 C. milk
1 egg
1/4 tsp. nutmeg
1/8 tsp. dried mint leaves
(crumbled)
1 onion, chopped

1 garlic clove, minced
1 plum tomato, chopped
1/8 tsp. salt
1/8 tsp. black pepper
12 oz. frozen spinach, thawed
and drained

Preheat oven to 375°F. Combine cottage cheese, milk, egg, 1/8 tsp. nutmeg and mint in blender. Sauté onion and garlic for 1 minute. Add tomatoes, salt, pepper, and remaining nutmeg and sauté 2 more minutes. Add spinach, stirring until liquid evaporates for 3-5 minutes. Pour into greased baking pan. Bake for 30 minutes.

## MANGO, PECAN & FETA CHEESE SALAD

1 head of lettuce
1 mango, peeled and cut into
cubes
1/2 C. toasted pecans
8 oz. feta cheese, crumbled

Dressing:
3 T. canola oil
1 T. wine vinegar
1 T. lemon juice
1 T. orange juice
1 tsp. mustard
Salt and black pepper

Place lettuce in a bowl. Add fruit, pecans and feta cheese. Mix dressing ingredients well. Pour dressing on salad and toss lightly.

## CHICKPEA SALAD

1 can chickpeas, drained
1 red pepper, chopped
1 green pepper, chopped
1 cucumber, chopped
1/2 C. grape tomatoes,
chopped
1/2 C. black olives, chopped

1 red onion, chopped
Juice of 1/2 lemon
3 T. olive oil
1 tsp. oregano
1/2 tsp. black pepper
1/2 C. feta cheese

Mix ingredients well and serve.

6

## CURRIED CAULIFLOWER SALAD

2 lbs. frozen cauliflower, thawed
   and drained
1/4 C. plain yogurt
2 T. mayonnaise

1/2 tsp. curry powder
1/8 tsp. salt
1/8 tsp. black pepper
2 tsp. parsley

Steam cauliflower for 4 minutes. Let cool. Mix yogurt and next 4 ingredients. Pour over cauliflower and toss gently to coat. Add parsley and toss again.

## CUCUMBER SOUP

1 cucumber, rinsed and cut into
   chunks
1/2 C. sweet Vidalia onions,
   chopped
1 qt. plain yogurt

Juice of 1 lemon
1 tsp. lemon zest
1 tsp. Tabasco sauce
1/2 tsp. salt
2 T. fresh dill or 2 tsp. dried dill

Puree all ingredients, except for the dill, in a blender or food processor. Chill. Garnish with dill.

## RATATOUILLE

1 onion, finely chopped
1 T. olive oil
2 cloves garlic, minced
1 large zucchini, diced
1/2 red bell pepper, diced
8 oz. can corn, drained

1 tomato, diced
1/2 tsp. cumin
1 tsp. salt
1/4 tsp. pepper
Shredded cheddar cheese

Sauté onion until it begins to brown. Add garlic and stir one minute until fragrant. Do not allow garlic to brown. Add zucchini, bell pepper and corn. Stir, cover and cook for about 10 minutes. Uncover, add tomato and cumin. Cook uncovered for 15 to 20 minutes. Add salt and pepper. Sprinkle with cheese.

# EASY, CHEESY SQUASH

6 yellow squash, sliced
1 medium onion
1 C. grated cheese

Salt and black pepper, to taste
Chopped fresh chives or parsley,
  for garnish (optional)

Sauté squash and onion, stirring occasionally, for about 4-5 minutes. Stir in cheese, stirring constantly, until cheese has melted, 1-2 minutes. Remove pan from heat, season with salt and pepper, and garnish with chopped chives or parsley, if desired.

# EZ ZUCCHINI

1/2 C. onion, sliced
2 zucchini, thinly sliced
1 T. water

1/2 tsp. salt
1/4 tsp. black pepper
2 T. grated Parmesan cheese

Sauté onion until translucent. Add zucchini and water. Reduce heat and cook until crisp tender. Add salt and pepper. Sprinkle with Parmesan cheese.

# CHEESY ZUCCHINI BAKE

3 medium zucchini, sliced
1 tsp. salt
8 oz. grated cheese (Swiss,
  mozzarella or cheddar)
1 onion, chopped
4 eggs, beaten

1 dash black pepper
1/2 tsp. oregano
1/2 tsp. basil
3 T. grated Parmesan cheese
1/4 C. vegetable oil

Combine all the ingredients in a bowl and mix well. Pour into a lightly greased baking dish and bake at 350°F for about 40 minutes, until slightly brown.

# CHEESY ZUCCHINI CRISPS

1/3 C. crushed cornflakes*
2 T. grated Parmesan cheese
1/2 tsp. salt
1/4 tsp. garlic salt

1/4 tsp. onion powder
1/8 tsp. black pepper
4 small zucchinis, cut in strips
1/4 C. butter, melted

Preheat oven to 375°. In a medium bowl, combine crushed cornflakes, Parmesan cheese, and spices. Mix until well incorporated. Dip zucchini strips in the melted butter and then into the cornflakes mixture. Place zucchini strips in a single layer on a baking sheet. Bake in oven for about 10 minutes, until crisp. Makes 4 to 6 servings.
*Cornflakes contain sweeteners and should not be used by those who are abstaining from sweeteners.

# CORN & ZUCCHINI MEDLEY

2 C. chopped zucchini
1 1/2 C. corn kernels
1 small onion, chopped

Pinch of pepper
1/4 C. shredded cheese

Sauté chopped zucchini, corn kernels and chopped onions until tender but crisp, about 10 minutes. Season with pepper. In a medium bowl, combine sautéed vegetables and shredded cheese.

# ITALIAN GREEN BEANS

1/3 C. olive oil
1 medium onion, diced
1 green pepper, diced
1 clove garlic, minced
1 lb. frozen cut green beans,
    thawed

1 tsp. dried basil
Salt and black pepper, to taste
1/3 C. grated Parmesan cheese

Preheat the oven to 350°F. Sauté onion until lightly browned. Add the green pepper and garlic, and sauté 2 more minutes. Stir in the green beans, basil, salt and pepper. Transfer to a baking dish and sprinkle with Parmesan cheese. Bake until the cheese has browned, about 10 minutes.

# CORN KUGEL

1 T. finely chopped onion
1 T. finely chopped green or red
    bell pepper
1 C. frozen or canned corn
1/4 tsp. nutmeg

Dash white or black pepper
1/4 C. milk
1/4 C. dry milk
1 egg
1 tsp. butter

Preheat oven to 325°F. In a medium-sized bowl, mix the onion, bell pepper, corn, nutmeg, and pepper. In a blender, combine the milk, dry milk, egg, and butter. Pour milk mixture over the corn mixture and toss to mix. Pour the entire mixture into a greased baking pan. Bake for 1 hour.

# BAKED EGGPLANT

1 C. onions, chopped
2 small eggplants
2 C. ricotta cheese

1 tsp. basil
1 tsp. oregano
1 C. crushed tomatoes

Sauté onions until brown. Peel eggplants, slice thinly and soak in salt water for 10-15 minutes to remove bitterness. Rinse well.
Mix basil, oregano, crushed tomatoes and sautéed onions.
Place eggplant in a single layer in a greased baking dish, then layer with ricotta cheese, then top with layer of tomato mixture. Bake at 350°F for 45 minutes.

# FLORENTINE SQUASH BAKE

2 T. arrowroot
1/8 tsp. cayenne pepper
2 C. milk
1/2 C. onion, chopped
3 garlic cloves, minced

10 oz. frozen chopped spinach,
    thawed, drained and
    squeezed dry
5 C. cooked spaghetti squash

Place arrowroot and cayenne pepper in a bowl. Gradually add milk, blending with a wire whisk until smooth.
Sauté onion and garlic for 1 minute. Add milk mixture and cook 6 minutes or until thickened, stirring constantly. Add spinach; stir well. Remove from heat and stir in squash. Pour mixture into greased baking dish. Bake at 375°F for 20 minutes.

# SPINACH FLORENTINE

1 lb. fresh spinach or 10 oz.
  frozen spinach
1 medium red onion, sliced
1 medium tomato, chopped
4 large mushrooms, sliced

1 T. butter
1 tsp. basil
1 tsp. oregano
1/2 tsp. black pepper
1/2 C. ricotta cheese

Wash spinach and cut stems off. Melt butter in large saucepan. Add basil, oregano, and pepper. Add vegetables to pan and simmer over medium heat, stirring occasionally until spinach becomes mushy. Add ricotta cheese and stir. Cook approximately 10 minutes.

# SAUTEED VEGETABLES WITH RICOTTA

1 C. low fat ricotta cheese
1 C. tomatoes, chopped
1/2 C. bell peppers, chopped
2 garlic clove

1 T. olive oil
Salt
Pepper
Basil

Sauté vegetables in oil. Stir in ricotta cheese and spices. Serve over brown rice or quinoa.

# CREAMY VEGETABLE CASSEROLE

1 onion, diced
1 can unsweetened corn,
  drained
1 can sliced mushrooms, drained
2 C. cottage cheese
1 C. plain yogurt
1 tsp. baking soda

1 tsp. baking powder
4 eggs
1/2 C. oat bran
1/2 tsp. salt
1/8 tsp. black pepper
1/2 tsp. basil
1/4 tsp. thyme

Sauté onion until golden brown. Mix all ingredients well. Pour into a greased baking pan and bake at 350°F for 1 hour.

# VEGGIE PARMESAN

1 pkg. frozen mixed vegetables
1/2 C. onion, diced
1/2 C. green pepper, diced

1 C. marinara sauce
3 T. grated Parmesan cheese, divided

Preheat oven to 350°F. Spray a large casserole dish with nonstick spray and layer the mixed vegetables, onion, and pepper. Mix the marinara sauce with 2 T. of Parmesan cheese and pour it over the vegetables. Cover and bake for 1 hour. Uncover, sprinkle with remaining Parmesan cheese and continue to bake for 10 minutes, or until the liquid thickens and the mixture bubbles.

# BAKED FALAFEL

1 medium potato, peeled
1 T. dried parsley
2 small onions, finely chopped
2 T. oil
2 cans garbanzo beans (chickpeas)
2 green onion (scallions), chopped

1 T. yogurt
1/4 tsp. garlic powder
2 tsp. salt
2 dashes chili pepper
Black pepper, to taste
1/4 tsp. paprika

Preheat oven to 350°F. Boil and mash potato. Grind chickpeas in food processor. Sauté onions until translucent, then add green onions and parsley. Mix onions with chickpeas and other ingredients. Form into balls. Place on greased baking sheet and bake for 10 minutes on each side.

# CHEESE LATKES

1 C. cream cheese
1/2 C. cottage cheese
1 C. shredded zucchini
2 eggs

2 tsp. baking powder
2 tsp. vanilla extract
Small pinch of salt

Mix together all ingredients in a bowl by hand or with an immersion blender. Spray a frying pan with nonstick spray and drop the cheese mixture by small spoonfuls into pan. Fry on both sides until golden brown.

## FLUFFY BUTTERMILK MASHED POTATOES

3/4 lb. potatoes, peeled and
   boiled
1/4 C. warm buttermilk

2 tsp. butter
Sea salt
Black pepper, to taste

Mash the potatoes and warm buttermilk well. Stir in the butter and salt and pepper.


## MASHED POTATOES AND CAULIFLOWER

4 cloves garlic, minced
1 small onion, chopped
3/4 lb. (12 oz.) potatoes, peeled
1 lb. frozen cauliflower, thawed
   and drained
1/4 C. buttermilk

1/4 C. cottage cheese
2 tsp. butter
Salt and pepper, to taste
Grated Parmesan cheese

Sauté onion and garlic. Boil potatoes until tender. Steam cauliflower until tender. Combine all the ingredients and whip until fluffy. Sprinkle Parmesan over mashed potatoes.


## CRUNCHY POTATO BAKE

4 T. butter
4 large potatoes, peeled and
   sliced
3/4 C. crushed cornflakes*

1 C. shredded Cheddar cheese
1 tsp. salt
1 tsp. paprika

Preheat oven to 350°. Melt butter, either in microwave, saucepan or in the oven. Mix potato slices with butter and place in a baking pan. In a medium bowl, combine crushed cornflakes, shredded Cheddar cheese, salt and paprika. Mix well and sprinkle mixture over potatoes. Bake for 30 minutes or until potatoes are tender and topping is crispy. Makes 8 to 10 servings.
*Cornflakes contain sweeteners and should not be used by those who are abstaining from sweeteners.

## PIZZA WITH POTATO CRUST

6 potatoes, parboiled, sliced
16 oz. tomato sauce
2 C. mozzarella cheese,
shredded

Parmesan cheese, grated
Optional vegetables: spinach,
mushrooms, onions, olives, etc.

Preheat oven to 400°F. Spray a deep, round oven-proof dish with nonstick spray. Place a layer of potato slices, then sauce, then cheese. Repeat up to four times. Sprinkle with Parmesan cheese. Cover pan and bake for about 45 minutes. Uncover and bake until browned on top.

## POTATO PUFF

6 C. mashed potatoes
1 C. sour cream or plain yogurt
1 C. cottage cheese

1 T. onion, minced
Salt and pepper, to taste
2 T. butter, melted

Combine the potatoes, sour cream or yogurt, cottage cheese, onion, salt and pepper, and place into a greased 2-quart casserole. Pour on melted butter. Bake at 350°F for 1 hour or until puffed and golden.

## CHILI CON QUESO

1 onion, chopped
2 tomatoes, chopped
2 fresh jalapeno peppers,
chopped

1 T. olive oil
1 lb. cheddar cheese, grated
1/2 C. shredded Monterey Jack
cheese

In a medium skillet over medium heat, sauté chopped onions, chopped tomatoes and chopped jalapeno peppers in olive oil, until tender. Add shredded Cheddar cheese and shredded Monterey Jack cheese. Cook over low heat, until cheeses are melted. Serve with mini rice cakes or sliced raw vegetables.

# Soups

# &

# Salads

## BUTTERNUT SWEET POTATO SOUP

1 onion, chopped
1 celery stalk, chopped
2 sweet potatoes, peeled and diced
1 butternut squash, peeled, seeded, and thinly sliced

4 C. vegetable stock (Imagine Soup) or water
I tsp. dried thyme
1/2 tsp. dried sage
salt
black pepper

Sauté the onion and celery in a soup pot until softened, about 10 minutes. Add sweet potatoes, squash, vegetable stock or water, thyme and sage. Season with salt and pepper, cover and simmer. Puree the soup with an immersion blender or in a blender or food processor.

## BUTTERNUT APPLE SOUP

I onion, diced
2 butternut squash, peeled and cut in chunks
2 apples, diced
2 C. vegetable broth (Imagine Soup)

2 C. water
1/8 tsp. ground thyme
I tsp. salt
Dash of black pepper
I C. unsweetened soy milk

Sauté onion until golden. Add squash, apples, broth, water, and seasonings. Bring to a boil. Reduce heat to low and simmer for 45 minutes, covered, until squash is tender. Puree soup until smooth. Return to low heat and stir in soy milk.

## BUTTERNUT LENTIL SOUP

1 onion, diced
2 cloves garlic, minced
1 C. lentils, rinsed
1 butternut squash, peeled and cubed
Bay leaf

1 tsp. salt
6 C. water
2 tsp. curry powder
1 tsp. ground cumin
2 T. dried parsley

Sauté onion and garlic for 15-25 minutes. Mix onions and garlic in a large pot with lentils, butternut squash, bay leaf, salt, curry, cumin and water. Bring to a boil. Reduce flame and simmer approximately 45 minutes. Remove bay leaf and add parsley before serving.

## BUTTERNUT CAULIFLOWER SOUP

1 small onion, chopped
1 small butternut squash, peeled
and cut in chunks
1 bag frozen cauliflower

4 C. water
1/2 C. Old-Fashioned oats
Salt to taste
White pepper to taste

Combine all ingredients in pot. Bring to a boil. Reduce heat and simmer for 30 minutes. Puree in blender or with hand blender.

## GARLIC AND ACORN SQUASH SOUP

1 acorn squash, peeled and cut
in wedges
1 sweet potato, peeled and
cubed
1 potato, peeled and cubed
6 whole garlic cloves

1/2 tsp. salt
1 small onion, diced
6 C. chicken stock or water
Dash of pepper
Dash of cinnamon

Place vegetables in a pan with garlic cloves. Brush vegetables with olive oil and sprinkle with salt. Bake at 375°F for 45 minutes. In a pot, sauté onion. Add chicken stock or water and roasted vegetables. Simmer for 30 minutes. Puree in blender or use immersion blender. Add pepper and cinnamon.

## EASY BROCCOLI SOUP

2 lb. frozen broccoli, thawed
1 sweet onion
4 cups vegetable broth (Imagine
soup)
1 C. unsweetened soy milk

3 cloves garlic
2 tsp. salt
1/2 tsp. black pepper
2 T. olive oil

Combine all ingredients in pot and bring to a boil. Lower heat, cover, and simmer for 45 minutes. Blend with an immersion blender or in a food processor.

## EGG DROP SOUP

Chicken broth
4 eggs, lightly beaten

Salt to taste
A few drops of sesame oil

Heat chicken broth. Add a few drops of sesame oil to chicken broth. Very slowly pour in the eggs in a steady stream. To make shreds, stir the eggs rapidly in a clockwise direction for one minute. To make thin streams or ribbons, gently stir the eggs in a clockwise direction until they form.

## SMOOTH & HEARTY SPLIT PEA SOUP

4 qts. water
2 lb. split peas
6 cloves garlic, sliced in half
3 small onions, diced
7 carrots, peeled and sliced

7 celery stalks, chopped
3 bay leaves
1 T. salt
1/2 tsp. pepper

Boil water in a large pot. Rinse peas and add to pot. Add vegetables and spices. Bring soup to a boil, then lower to simmer for approx 1 1/2 to 2 hours. Remove bay leaves. Puree soup and veggies with an immersion blender or remove soup and blend in food processor or blender.

## VEGETABLE PEA SOUP

1/2 C. water
1/2 C. split peas
5 carrots
2 sweet potatoes
2 zucchini

2 parsnips
1 onion
1 tsp. salt
1 tsp. dried dill

Bring water to a boil. Lower heat and add peas. Cover and simmer for 1 hour. Peel and cut remaining vegetables into large chunks. Add vegetables, salt, and dill. Bring to a boil, then lower heat and simmer, covered, for 1 more hour. Puree with an immersion blender in the pot or in batches in a blender or food processor.

## ORANGE PUMPKIN SOUP

2 C. apples, sliced
2 cans of pumpkin
4 clementines, peeled

4 tangerines, peeled
6 C. water or chicken broth
Cinnamon

Place all ingredients in a pot. Cook over medium flame for 30-40 minutes until apples soften and mixture is "mushy." Use immersion blender to make smooth.

## LENTIL-VEGETABLE SOUP

5 C. water
1 sweet potato, peeled and
  chopped
1 C. lentils
2 onions, chopped

1/4 C. barley
2 T. dried parsley
2 carrots, chopped
1 celery stalk, chopped
2 tsp. cumin

Combine all the ingredients in a pot and simmer until the lentils are soft, about 1 hour.

## TOMATO VEGETABLE SOUP

1 leek, sliced
3 sweet potatoes, peeled and
  diced
3 carrots, sliced
3 parsnips, sliced
3 stalks of celery, sliced

3 bay leaves
1/2 tsp. oregano
1/2 tsp. basil
Salt to taste
1 large can of crushed tomatoes
15 oz. can diced tomatoes

Sauté leek in a little oil for 5-10 minutes. Add all other ingredients except the crushed and diced tomatoes. Add enough water just to cover all of the vegetables. Cook until everything is soft. Remove the bay leaves. For a smoother texture, puree the vegetables in a food processor, blender, or with an immersion blender. Add crushed tomatoes and diced tomatoes.

## THAI CARROT SOUP

1/8 C. olive oil
1 T. minced garlic
1-1/2 tsp. ground ginger
3 lbs. carrots, sliced
1 T. salt

1/2 tsp. white pepper
6-8 C. vegetable stock (Imagine Soup)
1 C. coconut milk, unsweetened

In large pot, heat the oil and sauté the garlic and ginger for 2 minutes (do not allow to brown). Add carrots, salt, and white pepper. Sauté for 5 minutes, stirring constantly. Add the vegetable stock and bring to a boil. Lower heat to a simmer and add the coconut milk. Cook uncovered for 1 hour, or until carrots are tender. Process using an immersion blender. Add extra stock if soup is too thick. Taste and adjust seasoning with salt and pepper.

## CARROT AND CAULIFLOWER SOUP

1 C. carrots, diced
1 C. potatoes, cubed
1/2 C. frozen cauliflower, thawed
5 C. water, divided
1/2 tomato, finely chopped

1/2 tsp. salt
1/8 tsp. pepper
1 tsp. sesame oil
1/2 tsp. dried ginger
1/4 C. fresh finely chopped cilantro or 2 T. dried cilantro

In a large soup pot over medium heat, combine carrots, potatoes, cauliflower and 3 cups water. Boil for 10 minutes and transfer to a blender or food processor. Puree vegetables and water and return to soup pot. Add remaining 2 cups water. Boil mixture over medium heat for 20 minutes. Add finely chopped tomato, salt, pepper, sesame oil and ginger. Boil for an additional 2 minutes. Garnish with cilantro.

# SWEET POTATO SOUP

2 lb. sweet potatoes, peeled and
    cubed
1 large butternut squash, peeled
    and cubed
1 large onion, sliced

1 qt. water
2 tsp. cinnamon
1 tsp. allspice
1 tsp. ground cloves
2 C. applesauce, unsweetened

In large soup pot, sauté onions until soft. Add sweet potatoes, butternut squash and water, bring to a boil, then simmer covered for an hour. Blend soup with immersion blender. Add spices and applesauce, cooking for another 10 minutes.

## POTATO-ZUCCHINI SOUP

3 sweet onions, diced
3 potatoes, cubed
3 zucchinis, chopped
3 T. olive oil

6 C. water, or more as needed
Salt
Garlic powder
Black pepper

Sauté onion. Add potatoes, zucchini, water and spices to taste. Bring to a boil and then lower to a simmer for one hour. Mash mixture with a potato masher or blender to make soup smoother.

## BLACK BEAN SOUP

1 can black beans
1 qt. water
1 1/2 tsp. salt
1 T. olive oil
1 C. onions, chopped
1/2 C. green peppers, chopped

1 tsp. garlic, minced
1/2 tsp. ground cumin
1/2 tsp. oregano
1/8 tsp. dry mustard
1 1/2 tsp. lemon juice

Bring beans, water and 1 teaspoon salt to a boil. In a separate pan, sauté onions until tender and then stir in remaining ingredients. Combine vegetables with beans, cover and simmer for 1 hour, stirring occasionally.

## BEEF AND BARLEY SOUP

1 T. oil
1 lb. beef cubes
1 lb. soup bone
8 C. water
2 T. parsley
Salt and pepper, to taste
2 T. paprika

1 tsp. allspice
1 C. raw barley
1 C. celery, chopped
1 C. onion, chopped
1 C. carrots, chopped
1 C. fresh or canned tomatoes
Parsley for garnish

Put oil in pot on medium heat and lightly brown beef cubes and soup bone. Add water and bring to a boil, skimming surface as needed. Add remaining ingredients, reduce heat to low, cover and simmer for 1- 2 hours.

## MUSHROOM BARLEY SOUP

1 lb. mushrooms, sliced
2 garlic cloves, sliced
2-3 onions, diced
4 qts. water
2 pieces flanken or 4 marrow
   bones

6 carrots, sliced
2 stalks celery, chopped
Garlic powder
2 tsp. salt
1 C. raw whole barley

Sauté onions until golden, then add garlic and mushrooms. In a separate pot, bring flanken or bones and water to a boil, then simmer on low heat for 1 hour. Add carrots, celery, garlic powder, salt, barley and sautéed vegetables. Simmer an additional 1 hour.

## CREAMY BEET SOUP

2 15-ounce cans diced beets,
   undrained
2 C. unsweetened soy milk

4 T. apple juice concentrate
2 tsp. balsamic vinegar
1 tsp. dried dill

Blend ingredients in a blender until creamy. Pour into a pot and heat gently until hot.

# BANANA FRUIT SOUP

2 bananas
1 T. lemon juice
15 oz. can crushed pineapple, juice drained and reserved
1 C. ground almonds

1 C. unsweetened shredded coconut
10 dates, pitted
4 C. fruit juice

Puree the bananas, lemon juice, and half of the fruit juice. Then pulse this together with the nuts and transfer it all to a mixing bowl. Pulse the coconut and the pineapple together. Add to the bowl. Add in all remaining juices and mix together. Chill and serve in tall glasses.

# CORN SALAD

1 can yellow corn, no sugar added, drained
1 can white corn, no sugar added, drained
1 red bell pepper, diced
1 green bell pepper, diced

1 red onion, minced
1 T. dried parsley
1/2 tsp. garlic powder
1/2 tsp. salt
1/2 tsp. black pepper
2 T. olive oil

Combine ingredients and serve! Optional: Add 1 can of kidney beans or black beans drained and rinsed and a dash of chili powder.

# BLACK BEAN AND CORN SALAD

1 green pepper, chopped
16 oz canned or frozen corn, thawed
16 oz. can of black beans (well drained)
1/8 C. olive oil

1 small onion, finely chopped
2 plum tomatoes, chopped
1 tsp. curry powder
1/8 tsp. chili pepper
1 garlic clove, minced

Combine all ingredients and mix well.

# SPICY CORN SALAD

15 oz. can corn, drained
1/3 C. chopped red pepper
1 avocado, peeled and
    chopped
1/3 C. chopped onion

4 cloves garlic, minced
Dash of Tabasco sauce
3 T. apple cider vinegar
1/4 C. olive oil

In a medium bowl, combine corn, red pepper, avocado pieces, onion, garlic, Tabasco sauce, apple cider vinegar and olive oil. Toss until evenly incorporated. Chill in refrigerator until ready to serve. Makes 6 to 8 servings.

# ROASTED PEPPER AND CORN SALAD

3 C. frozen corn
2 T. olive oil
1/4 C. jarred roasted peppers or
    pimientos, chopped

1 scallion, chopped
1/4 tsp. salt
1 T. dried basil

Place the oil in a nonstick pan and heat. Add the corn and stir until nicely colored. Remove corn from pan. Mix corn, roasted peppers, spices, and scallions in a bowl. Refrigerate and serve cold.

# CARROT SALAD

6 carrots, sliced
1/4 C. olive oil
2 T. fresh lemon juice

2 cloves garlic, pressed
4 T. parsley, chopped
1/4 tsp. salt

Boil carrots in a small amount of salted water until tender, about 20 minutes. Drain and cool for a few minutes. Combine with remaining ingredients, tossing gently to coat. Chill before serving.

# CELERY SALAD

8 stalks of celery, sliced in thin
   sticks
3 carrots, shredded
1 red pepper, cut into thin strips
1 small red onion, cut into thin
   half circles

3 T. olive oil
3 T. vinegar
1/2 tsp. salt
1/2 tsp. garlic powder
3 T. dried parsley

Combine vegetables. Add dressing and serve.


# CALIFORNIA WALDORF SALAD

2 apples, diced
1 carrot, grated
1/2 C. raisins
1/4 C. walnuts, chopped

1/3 C. mayonnaise
3 T. rice vinegar (or apple cider
   vinegar)

Mix apples, carrots, raisins, and walnuts. In a separate bowl, mix mayonnaise and vinegar. Add to salad and stir. Chill before serving.


# PINEAPPLE WALDORF SALAD

1 C. pineapple chunks, fresh or
   unsweetened canned
3 C. apples, cut in chunks
1/3 C. raisins
1 stalk celery, chopped

1 C. carrots, thinly sliced
1/3 C. walnut pieces
1 C. mayonnaise
1/4 C. green pepper, thinly sliced

Combine all ingredients except mayonnaise. Blend with the mayonnaise. Serve plain or on lettuce leaves.


# EASY MANGO, AVOCADO AND ONION SALAD

2 ripe mangoes, cut in chunks
2 avocados, cut in chunks
1 small red onion, thinly sliced
1 small jicama (optional), cut in
   chunks

2 T. lemon juice
Salt

Mix ingredients.

## TOFU SALAD

12 oz. soft tofu, slightly mashed
1 C. celery, chopped
1 C. green pepper, chopped
1 C. cabbage, chopped

1 tsp. sesame oil
1 T. Dijon mustard
1/2 tsp. curry powder

Mix all ingredients.

## GARBANZO BEAN SALAD

1 C. garbanzo beans
1 tsp. olive oil
1 tsp. balsamic vinegar
1/2 lemon, juiced
Salt and pepper to taste

1/2 tsp. dried oregano
1/2 tsp. Dijon mustard
1/4 red onion, thinly sliced and
    then chopped
1 tomato, chopped

Mix all ingredients together. Marinate for at least 3 hours before serving.

## EDIBLE PEPPER BOWL

1 bell pepper
1 bunch of celery, sliced in 4"
    sticks

1 lb. carrots, sliced in 4" sticks
Chumus

Cut the pepper in half (from side to side). Clean out the seeds. The bottom half of the pepper is the "bowl". Cut the other half of the pepper into thin slices. Put chumus in the bottom of pepper "bowl". Place several celery sticks, carrot sticks, and pepper slices into the pepper bowl for dipping and surrounding it on the plate.

## MEDITERRANEAN TOMATO SALAD

3 plum tomatoes, diced
1/2 small red onion, diced
1 1/2 T. dill
4 mushrooms, diced
15 black olives, sliced

2 T. olive oil
1/3 tsp. salt
1/8 tsp. black pepper
1/2 tsp. Za'atar seasoning

Mix ingredients well.


## TOMATO AND WAX BEANS

1 lb. fresh yellow wax beans,
   washed and trimmed
1 clove garlic, crushed
1 T. olive oil

Salt and pepper, to taste
1/4 C. water
2 T. fresh basil, chopped
3 tomatoes, chopped

Steam wax beans, drain and cool. Combine all ingredients.


## BEET SALAD

3 medium beets
1 1/2 T. lemon juice
1 T. cider vinegar

1 T. apple juice concentrate*
1 tsp. ground mustard
1/2 tsp. dried dill

Wash and peel beets. Cut each beet in half, and each half into four
wedges. Steam beets until they are tender when pierced with a fork.
Mix lemon juice, vinegar, apple juice concentrate, mustard, and dill.
Add beets and toss to mix. Serve hot or cold.
*Apple juice concentrate is a sweetener and should not be used by
those who are abstaining from sweeteners.

# PORTOBELLO MUSHROOM SALAD

4 large portobello mushrooms, sliced
2 heads of romaine lettuce, chopped
I pt. grape tomatoes
1/2 red onion, sliced

DRESSING
1/3 C. olive oil
1/8 C. vinegar
1/2 tsp. garlic powder
1/2 tsp. salt
1/8 tsp. dry mustard
1/8 tsp. paprika

Sauté mushrooms for a few minutes, until tender. Mix the dressing ingredients in a separate bowl. Combine the salad ingredients in a large bowl and place mushrooms over salad before serving. Drizzle with dressing.

# GREEN BEAN AND MUSHROOM SALAD

2 C. green beans
1/2 C. mushrooms, sliced
1/2 C. red onion, chopped
3 T. olive or canola oil

1 T. balsamic or red wine vinegar
1 clove garlic, minced
1/2 tsp. salt
1/4 tsp. black pepper

Boil the green beans for 5 minutes. Drain and place the green beans immediately into a bowl of ice water. Drain green beans, add mushrooms and onions and toss to mix.
To make the dressing, whisk together the oil, vinegar, salt, pepper, and garlic.

# MUSHROOM SUGAR SNAP PEA SALAD

1/2 lb. fresh mushrooms, sliced
1 green onion (scallion), sliced
1 lb. sugar snap peas, diced
1/2 C. water chestnuts, sliced
1/4 C. balsamic vinegar
1/4 C. olive oil

1 tsp. dried parsley
3/4 tsp. dried basil
1/2 tsp. salt
1/2 tsp. pepper
Garlic powder

Combine mushrooms, green onions, and sugar snap peas. Combine vinegar and oil in a small bowl and whisk until blended. Stir in parsley, basil, salt, pepper, and garlic powder. Add to vegetable mixture and toss well.

# LENTIL SALAD

1 C. dry lentils, rinsed
2 C. water
1/4 tsp. salt
1/2 lb. green beans
Lettuce leaves, chopped
2 ripe plum tomatoes, cut into
   long wedges
1/2 C. bell pepper, diced

Dressing
2 T. cider vinegar
2 tsp. Dijon mustard
2 cloves garlic, crushed
1 tsp. ground ginger
1/4 tsp. salt
1/4 C. water
1 T. olive oil

Boil lentils in water and salt. Lower heat to simmer, partially covered for 20 minutes. Dressing: Whisk together vinegar, mustard, garlic, ginger and salt. Add 1/4 C. water and oil and mix well. Steam the green beans for 3 minutes. Drain well. Arrange green beans on plate with lettuce, peppers, and tomatoes; drizzle with half the salad dressing. Drain lentils and mix with remaining dressing. Mound lentils over salad vegetables.

# SALAD NICOISE

6 oz. can of tuna
2 hard-boiled eggs, sliced
2 baked potatoes
1 C. red onion, chopped
1 C. tomato, diced
2 C. lettuce
1/3 C. black olives
1 bell pepper, sliced

Vinaigrette:
1/2 T. scallion, finely minced
1/2 T. Dijon mustard
1/4 tsp. salt
1/2 T. freshly squeezed lemon
   juice
1/2 T. wine vinegar
1/3 C. olive oil
Black pepper

Peel potato and cut in cubes. Scatter chopped vegetables and egg on top of lettuce. Place tuna in center on top of greens. Arrange potato slices in circle around lettuce, following circumference of plate. Drizzle with vinaigrette.

## CHICKEN AND PEPPER SALAD

4 oz. chicken, cooked and cut
    into cubes
1 C. bell peppers, diced
2 T. olive oil
2 tsp. white vinegar

1/2 tsp. basil
1/4 tsp. oregano
1 clove garlic, minced
1 C. salad greens

In a medium bowl, gently stir together chicken and peppers. In a separate bowl, stir together olive oil, vinegar, basil, oregano and garlic. Pour dressing over chicken and peppers. Toss gently and serve on salad greens.


## CHICKEN TARRAGON SALAD

1/2 chicken, either baked or
    boiled
1 C. green grapes, halved
Onion powder

Garlic powder
Salt
Tarragon
2 T. mayonnaise

Remove skin and bone from the chicken and cut into 1/2-inch pieces. Combine chicken, grapes, salt, onion and garlic powder. Sprinkle with tarragon lightly, yet using more than the other spices. Add mayonnaise and mix.


## TURKEY POMEGRANATE SALAD

1 C. pineapple bits, drained
3 C. cooked turkey, diced
2 stalks celery, sliced
1 apple, diced

1/2 C. pomegranate seeds
1/2 C. toasted slivered almonds
1 C. mayonnaise
1/4 C. pineapple juice

Toss pineapple in large bowl with turkey, celery, apples, pomegranates seeds, and almonds. In separate bowl, combine mayonnaise and pineapple juice. Toss dressing with turkey mix. Garnish with additional pomegranate seeds and toasted almonds.

# WALNUT BARLEY SALAD

1/2 C. raw barley
1 1/2 C. water
Dressing:
1/4 C. lemon juice
1/4 C. olive oil
2 garlic cloves, minced
1/2 tsp. Dijon mustard
1 T. chopped fresh dill or 1 1/2 tsp. dried dill
1 tsp. salt

Black pepper, to taste
1 C. mushrooms, sliced
1 C. carrots, diced
1 C. green beans
1 C. red or yellow peppers, thinly sliced
1/2 C. fresh parsley, chopped or 3 Tbsp. dried parsley
2 tsp. margarine
2/3 C. walnuts, chopped

In a small pan on low heat, toast the barley until beginning to brown. Place the barley into boiling water. Lower heat, cover, and simmer until most of the water has been absorbed and the barley is soft, about 40 minutes. Drain any excess liquid.

While the barley cooks, mix all of the dressing ingredients. In a separate bowl, pour half of the dressing over the mushrooms and set aside.

Place the carrots in boiling water for about 1 minute. Remove from pot and boil the green beans for 4 minutes. Drain.

Mix barley with the remaining dressing. Combine barley with peppers, parsley, mushrooms, and carrots.

Toast the walnuts for 10 to 12 minutes, until golden and fragrant.

Just before serving, toss the green beans and walnuts into the salad.

## QUINOA SALAD

2 C. water or vegetable broth
1 C. quinoa
1 C. frozen green peas, thawed and drained
1 C. bell peppers (yellow, red and/or orange), diced
2 T. scallions or onions, chopped

Dressing
1 tsp. toasted sesame oil
1 tsp. olive oil
2 tsp. soy sauce
1/2 tsp. black pepper
1/2 tsp. salt

Bring water or broth to a boil. Add quinoa to boiling liquid; reduce heat and simmer, covered, for 15 minutes. Remove from heat and let stand, covered, for 5 minutes. Fluff with a fork. Cool to room temperature. Combine ingredients for dressing in small bowl and mix well. Stir into quinoa. Within 2 hours before serving, add peas, peppers, and scallions or onions to quinoa. Mix gently to combine. Serves 4.

## POTATO SALAD

2 medium potatoes, peeled and cubed
1/2 C. onion, diced
1/2 C. celery, diced
1/2 C. red bell pepper, finely diced
1 T. parsley

1 tsp. dill
1/4 C. mayonnaise
1 T. vinegar
1 1/2 tsp. Dijon mustard
1/8 tsp. salt
1/8 tsp. black pepper

Steam the potatoes until just barely tender when pierced with a knife, about 10 minutes. Do not overcook. Transfer to a large bowl and add the onion, celery, bell pepper, parsley, and dill. In a separate bowl, combine the mayonnaise, vinegar, mustard, salt, and pepper. Mix well. Add to the potato mixture and toss gently. Chill thoroughly before serving.

# SWEET POTATO SALAD

| | |
|---|---|
| 2 1/2. sweet potatoes | 1/8 tsp. black pepper |
| 1 T. Dijon mustard | 1 clove crushed garlic |
| 3 T. olive oil | 1/2 T. dried cilantro |
| 1/2 tsp. salt | |

Boil potatoes until tender. Let them cool and then peel and cut in cubes. Mix with remaining ingredients. Serve warm or at room temperature.

# AVOCADO OLIVE SALAD

| | |
|---|---|
| 3 avocados, cubed | Juice of half lemon |
| 2 C. grape tomatoes, halved | 1 T. mayonnaise |
| 1 can hearts of palm, sliced | Salt and pepper, to taste |
| 1/2 C. green olives, sliced | |

Mix gently until mayonnaise coats the whole mixture but not so much that the avocado pieces break down.

# AVOCADO SALAD

| | |
|---|---|
| 2 small avocados, chopped | 1/4 C. red onion, chopped |
| 1/2 C. red pepper, chopped | 10 olives, chopped |
| 1/4 C. green pepper, chopped | Juice of 1 lime |
| 1/4 C. carrot, diced | 1/2 tsp. salt |
| 1/4 C. cucumber, diced | Pepper, to taste |
| 1/4 C. tomato, chopped | Tabasco sauce, to taste |

Combine all ingredients, adding avocado last so that it won't get mashed.

## JALAPENO GUACAMOLE

3 avocados, peeled and pitted
1 small onion, finely chopped
4 cloves garlic, minced
1 medium tomato, chopped

3 T. lemon juice
1 small jalapeno pepper, chopped
Salt and pepper to taste

In a large bowl, place peeled and pitted avocados. Using a fork, mash avocados into a lumpy paste. Add chopped onion, minced garlic, chopped tomato, lemon juice and chopped jalapeno pepper. Mix well and season with salt and pepper to taste. Cover with plastic wrap and refrigerate until ready to serve. Serve with tortilla chips for dipping. Makes 8 servings.

## CHERRY TOMATO TOSS

4 C. halved cherry tomatoes
1/4 C. vegetable oil
3 T. cider vinegar
1 tsp. dried parsley flakes

1 tsp. dried basil
1 tsp. dried oregano
1/2 tsp. salt

In a small bowl, combine vegetable oil, cider vinegar, dried parsley flakes, dried basil, dried oregano, and salt. Mix well. In a medium serving bowl, place halved cherry tomatoes. Pour oil mixture over tomatoes and gently stir until coated. Chill in refrigerator at least 2 hours. Store in an airtight container and refrigerate until ready to serve. Makes 6 to 8 servings.

## TOMATO DIP

3 large overripe tomatoes
2 cloves garlic, minced
1 T. olive oil

1 tsp. cumin
2 tsp. salt
Chili pepper to taste

Puree tomatoes in blender. Add garlic, olive oil, salt, and pepper. Mix well.

# EASY GARLIC SALSA

14 1/2 oz. can diced tomatoes, drained
1/4 C. olive oil
1 T. minced garlic

1 T. fresh chopped parsley or 1 tsp. dried parsley
Salt and pepper to taste

In a medium bowl, combine drained tomatoes, olive oil, minced garlic, parsley, salt and pepper. Mix until well incorporated. Cover and chill.

# ITALIAN DRESSING

1 C. olive oil
1/2 C. red wine vinegar
1 tsp. garlic, chopped or 1/2 tsp. garlic powder

1 tsp. basil
1 tsp. oregano

Mix ingredients.

# TOMATO SALAD DRESSING

1 onion
2 C. tomato juice
1/2 C. lemon juice

Salt, pepper, garlic, parsley to taste

Grind ingredients in food processor or blender until smooth.

# NO SUGAR MAYONNAISE

2 raw eggs
1 tsp. salt
Dash of pepper

3 T. vinegar
3 C. oil

Blend eggs, salt and pepper in food processor very well for 5 minutes. Add vinegar and then very slowly add the oil while the processor is on.

# MOCK CHOPPED LIVER

1 onion, diced                    3 medium eggplants
1 can mushrooms, sliced           Salt and black pepper, to taste

Pierce eggplants several times with a fork. Bake at 400°F for 1 1/2 hours.
Sauté onions until golden brown. Add mushrooms and continue to sauté.
Scoop out inside of eggplant and mix with onions and mushrooms.
Blend with a hand blender or food processor.
Freezes well.

# NOTES

# Vegetables

## GREEN BEANS AMANDINE

1 lb. green beans, fresh or frozen     Water
1/2 C. techina     Roasted almonds, slivered

Trim the green beans, and break or cut the larger pieces in half. Place in steamer basket and steam until fork-tender. Rinse under cool water to stop the cooking process, and let drain completely. Place in an attractive serving dish and set aside.
Add just enough water to the techina to give it a runny, salad dressing consistency. Pour over steamed beans and toss gently to coat. Scatter almonds over the beans. Serve warm.

## GREEN BEANS AND WATER CHESTNUTS

1 T. oil     1 tsp. salt
2 medium onions, diced     Dash of onion powder
1 can water chestnuts, drained     5 shakes garlic powder
20 oz. frozen French-cut green
    beans

Sauté onions in oil until golden. Add remaining ingredients and sauté for about 20 minutes.

## GARLIC GREEN BEANS

1 lb. fresh green beans, ends     2 tsp. olive oil
    snapped     1/2 tsp. garlic salt

Rinse the green beans, put them in a microwave-safe container and cover. Microwave at full power for 3-5 minutes. Toss with the oil and garlic salt.

## GREEN BEAN STUFFING

1 pkg. frozen French-cut green
   beans
1 pkg. frozen cauliflower, thawed,
   drained, and mashed

1 lb. mushrooms, sliced
1 onion, chopped
Vegetable broth (Imagine Soup)
Soy sauce

Sauté onion, green beans, and mushrooms in a small amount of broth and soy sauce. Add cauliflower and cook until heated. Stuff into poultry.

## SESAME GREEN BEANS

1 lb. green beans
1 garlic clove, minced
2 T. toasted sesame seeds
5 T. soy sauce

1 tsp. sesame oil
1/4 tsp. salt
1/4 tsp. black pepper

Mix all ingredients. Bake in a greased baking pan at 425°F uncovered for approximately 15 minutes.

## BROCCOLI SPINACH SOUFFLÉ

1 lb. frozen broccoli, thawed and
   drained
1 lb. frozen spinach, thawed and
   drained
1/4 C. oat bran
1 C. boiling water
1 small onion

1 garlic clove
4 eggs
2 T. mayonnaise
1-1/4 tsp. salt
1 tsp. white pepper
1/2 tsp. ground rosemary
   (optional)

Preheat oven to 375°F. Mix oat bran and boiling water. Cover with aluminum foil immediately and let stand for 10 minutes.
Puree onions and garlic in food processor. In a large mixing bowl, mix onions, garlic, oat bran, spinach, and broccoli. In another bowl, mix eggs, mayonnaise, salt, pepper, and rosemary. Combine all ingredients and mix well. Bake uncovered in a greased baking dish for 45 minutes.

# INDIAN CAULIFLOWER

1 lb. frozen cauliflower
1 small tomato, finely chopped
1 tsp. ground cumin
1/2 tsp. ground coriander

1/2 tsp. ground ginger
Salt and pepper
Olive oil

In a large pan, heat oil over medium flame. Add cumin, coriander, and ginger. Cook spices until fragrant, about one minute. Add tomato and cauliflower florets to skillet. Gently mix until cauliflower is evenly coated with spice mixture. Add 1/4 C. water. Cover and cook 20 minutes until cauliflower is tender. Season with salt and pepper.

# CAULIFLOWER KUGEL

1 pkg. frozen cauliflower, thawed
   and drained
2 onions

Salt
Paprika

Puree the cauliflower, onions, and salt until creamy smooth. Put in greased baking pan and sprinkle with paprika. Bake at 400°F until browned on top.

# MASHED CAULIFLOWER

1 lb. frozen cauliflower florets,
   thawed and drained
1/8 to 1/4 C. unsweetened soy
   milk

1 T. margarine
Salt and pepper to taste
Paprika
Garlic

Place cauliflower pieces in the blender, then add soy milk, margarine, salt, and pepper. Whip until smooth. Pour cauliflower into a small baking dish. If desired, sprinkle with paprika and seasonings. Bake in a hot oven until bubbly or heat quickly in the microwave.
VARIATION: For children who eat only white foods, white rice can be added as well as potato.

# CAULIFLOWER LATKES

2 lb. frozen cauliflower, thawed, drained, and mashed
2 eggs
2 egg whites
1 small onion
1 clove garlic or 1/2 tsp. garlic powder
1/2 tsp. onion powder
2 T. oat bran
Salt and pepper, to taste
1 T. olive oil

Place eggs, onion, garlic, oat bran, oil, and seasonings in food processor, using the S-blade. Stir egg mixture with cauliflower. Spray a pan with nonstick cooking spray. Allow to heat up and drop batter by tablespoonfuls into hot pan. Fry on medium flame for 2-3 minutes on each side. Let them brown before flipping so that they do not fall apart. With each new batch, spray the pan with nonstick cooking spray.
Can be kept in a warm oven at 100° F.
Variation: Substitute broccoli or spinach instead of cauliflower.

# ROASTED CAULIFLOWER

1/4 C. olive oil
1/8 tsp. turmeric
2 garlic cloves, minced
Salt and pepper, to taste
1 lb. frozen cauliflower, thawed and drained

Preheat the oven to 400°F. Mix the oil, turmeric, fresh garlic, salt, and pepper in a large mixing bowl. Stir in the cauliflower florets and mix until they are evenly coated. Place the cauliflower in a single layer on a greased baking sheet and bake for 30 minutes until the cauliflower is brown.

## BEETS IN DILL SAUCE

4 C. beets, peeled and sliced
2 T. lemon juice
1 T. ground mustard
1 T. cider vinegar

1 T. apple juice concentrate
1 tsp. dried dill, or 1 T. fresh dill, chopped

Steam beets over boiling water until tender when pierced with a fork, about 20 minutes. Mix lemon juice, mustard, vinegar, apple juice concentrate, and dill. Add beets and toss to mix. Serve immediately or chill before serving.

## BRAISED BEETS

4 medium beets, washed, but
    not peeled or trimmed
2 T. balsamic vinegar

1 tsp. dried dill
Salt and pepper

Preheat oven to 400°F. Wrap the beets individually in foil, sprinkling 1 T. water on each before sealing the foil. Bake for 1 hour or until tender all the way through. The peel slips off easily once they are cooked. Sprinkle with balsamic vinegar, dill, salt and pepper.

## STEAMED CARROTS

1 lb. carrots
1 T. olive oil or margarine
1/2 tsp. lemon juice
Dash of dill

Dash of parsley
1/4 tsp. salt
Dash of marjoram (optional)

Place the carrots in a steaming basket with 2 inches of water in the pot below. Bring the water to a boil and steam over a high heat for approximately 12 minutes. Mix carrots with olive oil, lemon juice and spices.

# SAUTEED CABBAGE

1 bag cabbage, shredded          Salt and pepper, to taste
1 onion, diced                           Dry mustard

Sauté onions for 5 minutes. Then add cabbage and spices and sauté on low heat for about an hour, stirring approximately every 15 minutes. Add mustard when done.

# FRIED CABBAGE

3 T. olive oil                                Salt and pepper to taste
1 lb. shredded cabbage            4 1/2 oz. can mushrooms with
1 C. chopped celery                      liquid, optional
1 green bell pepper, diced         1 small onion, chopped

Sauté shredded cabbage, chopped celery, diced green pepper, salt, pepper, sliced mushrooms with liquid and chopped onions. Cover skillet and steam for about 15 to 20 minutes, stirring occasionally. Makes 6 servings.

# RED CABBAGE WITH APPLES

1 T. onion, chopped fine           1/2 C. water
2 Granny Smith apples, thinly    1 head red cabbage, shredded
   sliced                                       1 tsp. salt
2 T. lemon juice                         1/4 tsp. caraway seeds (optional)

Sauté onion until golden. Stir in remaining ingredients. Cover tightly and simmer over low heat for 15-20 minutes, stirring occasionally.

# CABBAGE MARINARA

1 lb. cabbage, shredded           Salt and pepper, to taste
1 lb. tomatoes, chopped           2 T. parsley
8 oz. tomato sauce                    2 T. oregano
1 tsp. basil

Mix ingredients and microwave covered for about 7-10 minutes. If you prefer, you can sauté ingredients instead of using the microwave.

## CHINESE CELERY AND CABBAGE

1 lb. cabbage, shredded
2 sticks celery, sliced thin

1 tsp. salt
1/2 tsp. dried ginger

Sauté cabbage for 3 minutes, stirring all the time. Add the salt, mixing well. Add celery and ginger to the cabbage with 2 T. water. Cook on high flame stirring all the while for about 2 minutes.


## MUSHROOM MEDLEY

Portobello mushrooms
Shiitake or oyster mushrooms
2 red peppers
1 red onion
2 small zucchini

1 eggplant
Parsley
Salt and pepper
Garlic powder

Preheat oven to 400°F. Slice all the vegetables thinly. Lay them out in a single layer on several greased cookie sheets, spray the vegetables with cooking spray and sprinkle with spices. Bake until slightly browned.


## ONIONS AND MUSHROOMS

4 onions, sliced
1 box fresh mushrooms
Salt

Pepper
Garlic powder

Slice onions and sauté. When onions are transparent, add mushrooms and spices. Keep flame low and stir occasionally.

# ZUCCHINI-STUFFED PORTOBELLO MUSHROOMS

4 large Portobello mushrooms, cleaned and dried, stems removed
3 small zucchini, unpeeled, scrubbed and shredded and drained
1 tsp. olive oil

1 clove garlic, minced
1 T. dried oregano
2 tsp. dried thyme
2 tsp. dried basil
Salt and pepper, to taste
1 egg
1 C. canned diced tomato

Preheat oven to 400°F. Arrange mushrooms stems side up on greased baking sheet. Spread 2 T. of diced tomato on top of each mushroom cap. Sauté garlic until translucent. Add zucchini and spices, and cook on medium heat for 5 minutes, or until zucchini is softened. Stir zucchini mixture with the remaining diced tomato. Spread zucchini tomato stuffing over the mushroom caps. You may top with grated cheese. Bake for 20-25 minutes until browned on top.

## ZUCCHINI STICKS

8 small zucchini
Basil
Garlic powder
Salt

Black pepper
Grated Parmesan cheese (optional)

Wash zucchini well. Cut unpeeled zucchini into sticks. Place zucchini in greased pan, spray with nonstick spray, and liberally sprinkle on spices. Sprinkle with Parmesan cheese, if desired. Broil on top oven rack until slightly crisp.

## ZUCCHINI AND GREEN APPLE

1 large onion, sliced
5 small zucchini, sliced
1 Granny Smith apple

1 large beefsteak tomato, diced
1/2 tsp. salt
1/4 tsp. black pepper

Peel and core apple. Slice apple into quarters and then slice half moon shapes. In large frying pan, sauté onion until golden brown. Add remaining ingredients, lower flame and simmer for 35-50 minutes.

44

## SAUTEED ZUCCHINI, PEPPER, AND TOMATOES

1 large onion, chopped
4 zucchinis, diced
2 green peppers, diced
2 red peppers, diced

4 large tomatoes, diced
2 garlic cloves, whole
Salt

Sauté onion until golden. Add remaining ingredients and sauté on medium heat for 1-1/2 hours. Stir continuously.

## QUICK SQUASH

3 plum tomatoes, chopped
2 garlic cloves, chopped
1 tsp. dried parsley
1/2 tsp. oregano

3 yellow squash, sliced
Salt and pepper, to taste
1/4 C. tomato juice

Combine all ingredients. Cover and microwave on high for 3 minutes. Stir, then microwave for 3 more minutes. If you prefer, you can sauté ingredients instead of using the microwave.

## BUTTERNUT SQUASH

2 butternut squash
Salt

Pepper
Garlic powder

Using a very sharp knife, slice squash in half the long way. Scoop out the seeds and place halves, sliced side up in a greased baking pan. Sprinkle with salt, pepper and garlic powder. Bake at 450°F for 30 minutes, or until the skin is crispy and the sliced sides are caramelized.

# SPAGHETTI SQUASH LATKES

| | |
|---|---|
| 1 spaghetti squash | 1/4 C. oat bran |
| 1 onion, grated | 1 1/2 tsp. salt |
| 2 eggs | 1/2 tsp. black pepper, to taste |

Pierce squash in several places with knife or fork. Cook whole squash for about 10 minutes in microwave, until tender. Alternatively, you can slice spaghetti squash in half and remove seeds. Place spaghetti squash face up in a baking pan. Bake for 1 hour at 450°.
Let squash cool for several minutes, then remove seeds and scoop out squash. Mix with remaining ingredients. Coat skillet with vegetable spray or oil and drop mixture by spoonful into pan. Brown well on both sides.

# SPAGHETTI SQUASH WITH BELL PEPPER SAUCE

| | |
|---|---|
| 1 spaghetti squash | 2 cloves garlic, minced |
| 4 red peppers, chopped | 1 C. marinara sauce |
| 1 onion, chopped | |

Pierce squash in several places with knife or fork. Cook whole squash for about 10 minutes in microwave, until tender. Alternatively, you can slice spaghetti squash in half and remove seeds. Place spaghetti squash face up in a baking pan. Bake for 1 hour at 450°.
Let squash cool for several minutes, then remove seeds and scoop out squash. Sauté bell pepper, onion and garlic for 7 minutes or until crisp-tender. Add marinara sauce and cook until heated. Pour pepper sauce over spaghetti squash.

# SPAGHETTI SQUASH CURRY

| | |
|---|---|
| 1 spaghetti squash | 1 T. curry powder |
| Salt and pepper, to taste | 1/2 T. cumin |
| Garlic powder and onion powder, to taste | |

Preheat oven to 450°F. Slice spaghetti squash in half and remove seeds. Place spaghetti squash face up in a baking pan. Add spices and roast for 1 hour until brown or crispy on edges and tender when pierced with a fork. Scrape inside of squash with tines of a fork to remove spaghetti-like strands.

## MARINATED EGGPLANT

4 eggplants
3 onions, diced
1 red pepper, diced

Salt and pepper
1 T. white vinegar

Cut eggplant into chunks - do not peel. Sauté onion, pepper, eggplant, salt and pepper until tender. Turn heat off, add vinegar, mix well, and let sit covered for 1 hour.
Freezes well.

## SMOTHERED EGGPLANT

1 medium eggplant, peeled and
   cubed
1 tsp. salt
1 medium onion, chopped

1 green pepper, chopped
1 garlic clove, minced
Black pepper

Put the eggplant into a large bowl, cover with warm water, add 1 tsp. salt and let soak for 20 minutes. Drain eggplant. Sauté onion until golden. Add eggplant, pepper, garlic, salt and black pepper. Sauté for a few more minutes, then cover and cook on medium-low heat for 10 minutes.

## BAKED EGGPLANT AND TOMATOES

1 eggplant
8 oz. can diced tomatoes
1/4 tsp. garlic powder

1/4 tsp. dried marjoram leaves
1 tsp. salt

Heat oven to 375°F. Peel and slice eggplant into 1/2-inch slices. Sauté Cook in boiling salted water for 5 minutes. Drain. Mix together tomatoes, marjoram, salt, and garlic powder. In a greased baking pan, place a layer eggplant and then a layer of tomato mixture. Repeat layers and bake for 20 minutes.

# MILLET STUFFED PEPPERS

2 C. water
1 C. millet
3 large carrots, shredded
1 small zucchini or yellow squash, shredded
1 C. soft tofu, drained
28 oz. can crushed tomatoes
1 tsp. fennel

1/2 tsp. anise seed
1/2 tsp. basil
1/2 tsp. garlic powder
2 T. soy sauce
1 tsp. parsley
Black pepper, to taste
2 T. onion flakes
6 green peppers

Bring 2 C. water to boil and add millet. Cover and simmer on low heat. Let cook until tender. Mix millet with carrots, shredded zucchini, and tofu, 1/2 of the can of tomatoes, fennel, anise, basil, garlic powder, soy sauce, parsley, black pepper, and onion flakes. Stuff into green peppers that have been cut in 1/2 and seeded. Lay in baking pan. Pour remaining crushed tomato mixture over peppers. Bake at 325°F for 1 hour.

# BROILED PEPPERS

Green, yellow, red or orange peppers, sliced
Salt

Pepper
Garlic powder

Place pepper slices on greased pan. Spray peppers with non-stick spray and sprinkle with spices. Broil for 18 minutes.

# SAUTEED BELL PEPPERS

4 bell peppers (green, yellow, orange, red), sliced
8 garlic cloves, minced

Salt and pepper, to taste
1 T. dried basil
1 T. parsley

Sauté peppers until tender, about 5 minutes. Stir occasionally. Add garlic to peppers and stir again. Season with basil, parsley, salt and black pepper.

## PORTUGUESE PEPPERS

3 T. olive oil
4 bell peppers, cut into thin strips
1 medium onion, finely chopped
1 T. finely chopped garlic

Salt and pepper
1/2 C. tomato sauce
1/4 tsp. saffron or 1/2 tsp. turmeric

Sauté the peppers, onions, garlic, salt, and pepper for about 3 minutes or until crisp and tender. Add tomato sauce and saffron or turmeric. Cover and simmer 15 minutes.


## SPICY ROASTED EDAMAME

1 1/4 C. frozen shelled
  edamame (green soybeans),
  thawed
2 tsp. olive oil
1/2 tsp. chili powder

1/4 tsp. dried basil
1/4 tsp. onion powder
1/4 tsp. ground cumin
1/8 tsp. paprika
1/8 tsp. ground black pepper

Preheat oven to 375°F. Mix ingredients. Spread in a greased baking pan or cookie sheet in a single layer. Bake uncovered until the beans begin to brown, about 12-15 minutes. Stir once halfway through cooking.


## RATATOUILLE

2 medium onions, sliced
1 garlic clove, minced
2 small zucchini, thinly sliced
2 small eggplants, peeled and
  cubed
2 green peppers, sliced

5 medium tomatoes, quartered
  or 2 C. canned diced
  tomatoes
1 tsp. dried basil leaves
2 T. parsley
1 tsp. salt
1/4 tsp. ground pepper

Sauté onions and garlic for 5 minutes. Add zucchini, eggplant and green pepper and sauté for 10 more minutes. Stir in tomatoes, basil, parsley, salt, and pepper. Reduce heat, cover and simmer for 15 minutes.

## PARSNIP POTPOURRI

5 zucchinis, julienned     3 garlic cloves, minced
8 parsnips, julienned      Salt
6 carrots, julienned       Pepper
1 lb. fresh string beans

Place vegetables in greased baking pan. Spray vegetables with nonstick spray and sprinkle with garlic, salt, and pepper. Bake covered 2 hours at 350°F. Uncover and bake for another 1/2 hour.


## POPPED ONION DELIGHT

5 yellow squash, julienned     1/2 lb. snow peas
5 parsnips, sliced          1 bag purple pearl onions
4 carrots, sliced           1 bag white pearl onions
1 onion, thinly sliced
4 cans of whole button
   mushrooms

Place all vegetables, except for pearl onions, in greased baking pan and spray vegetables with nonstick spray. Bake uncovered at 375°F, mixing frequently for 2 hours. Add fresh snow peas and bake for another 30 minutes.
Boil pearl onions in water for 5 minutes. Drain and place in bowl with cold water and ice. Drain. Slice the root end of each onion and squeeze the onion. The onions should pop out of their peel. Mix onions into vegetables and turn oven off. Leave vegetables in still warm oven for 30 minutes.


## FALL HARVEST VEGETABLES

2 yams          Fresh rosemary, to taste
4 carrots       Dried oregano, to taste
3 parsnips      Salt and pepper, to taste
2 T. olive oil

Preheat oven to 350°F. Peel the vegetables and cut into small, thin pieces, and combine in a bowl with oil and spices. Bake uncovered for 1 hour. Makes 4-6 servings.

# VEGGIE CHIPS

Butternut Squash
Beets
Sweet Potatoes
Spices
For a sweet taste, use cinnamon
  and nutmeg

For a savory taste, use any
  combination of salt, garlic,
  onion powder, dill, parsley,
  rosemary, and thyme.

Peel the vegetables and slice very thinly with an extremely sharp knife, or use a food processor to slice them. Spray several cookie sheets with nonstick spray, lay the vegetable slices down in one layer, then spray the top of the vegetables with nonstick spray. Sprinkle lightly with either cinnamon and nutmeg for a sweet taste, or with any combination of salt, garlic, onion powder, dill, parsley, rosemary, or thyme for a more savory taste. Bake on 400°F until the vegetables just start to turn brown.

# RUTABAGA CHIPS

2 Rutabagas, peeled and sliced
  into wedges

Salt

Place rutabaga on greased cookie sheet, spray rutabaga with nonstick spray and sprinkle with salt. Bake covered at 400°F for 1 1/2 hours. Uncover and bake for an additional 30 minutes, until crispy.

# SAUTEED RAINBOW VEGETABLES

2 garlic cloves, minced
2 carrots, cut into thin strips
1 tsp. salt
1 tsp. lemon pepper seasoning
3 small zucchini, cut into thin
  strips

3 small yellow squash, cut into
  thin strips
1 red pepper, cut into thin strips
1/3 C. scallion, chopped
1 tsp. dried basil

Sauté garlic for 2 minutes. Add carrots, salt, and lemon pepper and sauté for 3 additional minutes. Add remaining ingredients and sauté for 4 more minutes.

## ROASTED COLORFUL VEGETABLES

1 onion, diced
1 package fresh mushrooms,
   diced
Olive oil
16 oz. frozen French-style green
   beans

1 red pepper, sliced
1 orange pepper, sliced
1 can baby corn, chopped
1 T. onion flakes
1 T. kosher salt

Combine the onion and mushrooms in a greased baking pan and sprinkle with oil. Bake uncovered at 450°F for 25 minutes. Add the remaining vegetables, onion flakes and kosher salt. Mix well. Bake for another 10-15 minutes.

## VEGETABLE LOAF

1 large eggplant
2 medium onions, chopped
2 T. dried parsley
2 tomatoes, diced
1 celery stalk, diced
1 green pepper, chopped
1 C. scallions, chopped

1 egg beaten
1/2 C. oatmeal
1 tsp. oregano
4 T. oat bran
1 garlic clove, minced or 1 tsp.
   garlic powder
1/2 tsp. salt

Heat oven to 350°F. Peel and chop eggplant fine or grind in food processor. Sauté eggplant, onions, parsley, tomatoes, celery, green pepper and scallions. Transfer to mixing bowl and let cool. Add egg, 1/3 C. oatmeal, oregano, oat bran, minced garlic or garlic powder, and salt. Place in greased baking pan. Sprinkle with remaining oatmeal. Bake for 25 minutes.

## MEXICAN VEGGIES

1/2 onion, chopped
1 garlic clove, minced
1 red pepper, chopped
1 - 14.5 oz. can diced tomatoes
  with juice, or 1-2 fresh
  tomatoes, chopped
2 zucchini, sliced

2/3 C. unsweetened corn (frozen
  or canned)
1 small eggplant, peeled and
  sliced
Salt and pepper, to taste
1 tsp. cumin
1 tsp. cilantro

Sauté onion, garlic, and peppers until the onions are translucent. Add remaining ingredients and simmer for 15 minutes, stirring occasionally.

## NO SUGAR KETCHUP

1 C. unseasoned tomato sauce
1/2 tsp. dry mustard
1 tsp. vinegar

Dash of black pepper
1/2 tsp. garlic powder
1 tsp. soy sauce

Bring all ingredients to a boil, reduce heat and simmer for 10 minutes, stirring constantly.

## EASY TOMATO SAUCE

12 oz. canned tomato paste
12 oz. water
1 tsp. salt
1 tsp. onion powder
1 tsp. basil

1 tsp. oregano
1/8 tsp. black pepper
1/8 tsp. garlic powder
1 T. baby food jar of mixed
  vegetables

Mix all ingredients and simmer for 30 minutes.

# SAUTÉED LEEKS

2 large bunches leeks        5 cloves garlic, minced
1 large onion, diced          1 T. kosher salt

Scrub and rinse leeks very well. Dice leeks, both the dark green leaves and the white root into small pieces. Sauté all ingredients together until golden brown.

# Fish

## FRIDAY NIGHT SAUCY GEFILTE FISH

1 frozen gefilte fish loaf
Half a bag of baby carrots
2 stalks of celery, chopped

1 onion, chopped
1 bell pepper, chopped
1 jar of marinara sauce

Remove the paper wrapping from the fish (it's easier if it's slightly defrosted). Place gefilte fish loaf in a baking pan. Place vegetables on top and around the fish, then pour tomato sauce over it. Cover and bake at 350°F for 1 - 2 hours. Place on the blech before Shabbos and serve warm.

## SALSA GEFILTE FISH

2 T. oil
1 large onion, sliced
1 C. salsa

1/2 C. water
1 loaf frozen gefilte fish

Sauté onions until translucent. Unwrap frozen gefilte fish and place on top of onions. Mix the salsa and water together and pour over fish and onions. Simmer covered and cook for 1 - 2 hours. Can be served cold or hot.

## ROAST SALMON WITH VEGETABLES

1 lb. small red potatoes, halved
1/2 lb. mushrooms
3 T. olive oil
Salt and black pepper

1 lb. skinless salmon fillet
1 T. red wine vinegar
1 T. mustard
2 T. dried parsley

Heat oven to 400°F. Mix potatoes, mushrooms, 1 T. of olive oil, and 1/2 tsp. of salt and pepper in a baking pan. Bake for 20 minutes.
Place the salmon in the baking pan with the vegetables. Sprinkle salmon with 1/4 tsp. salt and pepper. Bake uncovered for approximately 12 to 15 minutes.
Mix the vinegar, mustard, parsley, 2 T. of olive oil, and 1/4 tsp. salt and pepper. Drizzle over the salmon and vegetables before serving.

## SALMON OR TUNA QUICHE (DAIRY)

1 C. sour cream
1 C. mayonnaise
1/4 C. water
1 T. lemon juice
1/4 C. fresh dill, chopped or 1 T. dried dill
1 tsp. garlic powder

3/4 tsp. salt
1/4 tsp. pepper
6 eggs, beaten
1 T. olive oil
2 onions, chopped
16 oz. canned boneless, skinless salmon or tuna, drained

Preheat oven to 375°F. Mix sour cream, mayonnaise, water, lemon juice, dill, garlic powder, salt and pepper. Pour one cup of the sauce into a bowl and refrigerate the remaining sauce. Mix the eggs into the one cup of sauce.
Sauté onions until golden brown. Add onions to the sauce. Mix salmon or tuna into the sauce. Pour mixture into a greased pie pan. Bake 30 minutes, until set. Serve warm or room temperature and drizzle with remaining dill sauce.

## SALMON OR TUNA LOAF (DAIRY)

1 C. oat bran
1/2 C. hot milk
32 oz. canned salmon or tuna, flaked
1 1/2 tsp. salt

1 1/2 tsp. paprika
1 tsp. lemon rind (optional)
2 T. lemon juice
2 eggs
2 tsp. hot sauce

Combine oat bran and milk. Let soak for 10 minutes. Add all other ingredients and mix lightly. Pour into a greased loaf pan. Bake 1 hour at 325°F.

## BAKED SALMON STEAKS

1 T. cooking oil
1 T. lemon juice
1/2 tsp. ground ginger

Salt and pepper
1 lb. salmon steaks

Mix oil, lemon juice, ginger, salt and pepper. Brush mixture on salmon, refrigerate for 1-2 hours. Bake salmon uncovered at 400°F until it flakes easily, about 10-15 minutes.

56

## GRILLED LIME SALMON

3 T. olive oil
1 tsp. fresh lime juice
1 T. dried marjoram
1/8 tsp. salt

1/8 tsp. black pepper
1 1/2 lb. salmon steaks
1 lime, cut into wedges

Mix oil, lime juice, marjoram, salt, and pepper. Brush the salmon steaks with the mixture. Set up a grill or preheat a broiler. Position the fish about 4 inches from the heat source and grill or broil the steaks for about 3 minutes per side until the fish flakes easily, brushing with more of the lime juice mixture after turning the fish. Decorate each serving with lime wedges.

## SALMON OR TUNA CROQUETTES

4 T. mayonnaise
2 T. dried dill
2 eggs
1/2 C. onion, finely diced
1/2 C. green pepper, finely diced

2 cans boneless, skinless salmon or tuna
2/3 C. oat bran
4 T. olive oil

Mix mayonnaise, dill, egg, onion, pepper and dill. Combine salmon or tuna with mixture and form into balls. Roll balls in oat bran and gently flatten into patties. Fry in oil for 3 minutes on each side.

## BROILED SALMON

1 C. soy sauce
1/2 tsp. ground ginger
1/2 tsp. black pepper

1 tsp. dried parsley
1 lemon
2 lb. salmon steaks or fillets

Mix soy sauce, ginger, black pepper, parsley, and juice from the lemon. Pour mixture over salmon. Place baking pan on top rack of the oven and broil for about 5 minutes per side.

## TUNA QUICHE (DAIRY)

I can tuna
2 stalks celery, sliced
2 T. green pepper, diced
(optional)
2 T. onions, diced

1/2 C. mayonnaise
2 eggs
8 oz. shredded cheese
4 oz. can sliced mushrooms,
drained

Combine all ingredients and pour into a greased pie pan. Bake at 400°F for 30 minutes.

## TUNA WITH BLACK PEPPER, ARTICHOKES, AND LEMON

1/2 red onion, thinly sliced
2 T. olive oil
18 oz. jarred artichoke hearts,
drained and halved
1 lemon, cut into 8 slices
2 cloves garlic, thinly sliced

1/2 tsp. dried thyme
1 1/2 lb. fresh tuna, cut into
1-inch cubes
1 1/2 tsp. salt
1 tsp. black pepper

Sauté onion in olive oil until softened, about 3 minutes. Add artichokes, lemon, garlic, and thyme. Sauté for 3 more minutes. Remove from pan. Season the tuna with salt and pepper. Heat the remaining oil in the skillet. Cook tuna, turning to brown on all sides for about 2 minutes. Toss tuna with artichoke mixture and serve over brown rice, kasha, or quinoa.

## TUNA PATTIES

1 C. zucchini, shredded
2 T. onion, chopped
1/2 tsp. garlic, minced
2 cans tuna, drained

2/3 C. oatmeal or oat bran
1/4 tsp. salt
1/4 tsp. pepper

Sauté zucchini, onion and garlic for 5 minutes. Mix with remaining ingredients. Form into patties and fry in large skillet over medium heat, about 3 minutes. Serve with lemon wedges.

# TUNA BURGERS

2 cans tuna
1/2 C. mayonnaise
2 onions, finely chopped
1/4 bell pepper, shredded
1/2 tsp. salt

1/2 tsp. black pepper
1-1/2 tsp. mustard
1 egg
2 tsp. dried parsley
1 small baked potato, peeled
and mashed

Mix all the ingredients. Shape mixture into 1 inch thick patties. Fry patties on one side for several minutes until bottom is browned (don't try to flip them too soon), then flip and brown other side.

# TUNA SQUARES

2 lbs. canned tuna
2 eggs or 4 egg whites
1/4 C. oat bran
2 T. lemon juice
1 red pepper, chopped

1 green pepper, chopped
1 onion, chopped or 3 green
onions, chopped
1 carrot, grated

Mix all ingredients together. Pour into a greased pan. Bake at 350°F for 25 minutes.

# LEMON TILAPIA

12 oz. tilapia
4 tsp. margarine
1/3 C. lemon juice
1 1/2 C. carrots, chopped

1/4 C. celery, chopped
1/4 C. green onion, chopped
2 tsp. dried parsley
2 lemons, thinly sliced

Melt margarine and mix with lemon juice, pepper, carrots, celery, onions and parsley. Place tilapia in baking dish and pour mixture over fish. Top fish with lemon slices. Wrap tightly in foil. Bake at 350°F for 20-30 minutes or until fish flakes easily.

## TILAPIA WITH VEGETABLES

1 lb. tilapia
1 C. mushrooms
1/2 C. celery
2 T. lemon juice

Oregano
Onion powder
Garlic powder

Preheat oven to 350°F. Place fish topped with vegetables and seasonings in baking pan. Wrap tightly with foil and bake for 20-30 minutes.

## VEGETABLE STUFFED TILAPIA

1 lb. tilapia fillets
1 zucchini
1/2 C. mushrooms
1 tomato
Salt and pepper, to taste

Pinch of chili pepper
Onion and garlic powder, to
   taste
2 tsp. margarine

Shred vegetables and seasonings in food processor. Lay fish in pan and place small amount of vegetable mixture on top of each fillet and top with 1/2 tsp. margarine each. Roll up fillets or fold end to end and fasten with a toothpick. Bake at 400°F for 20 - 30 minutes.

## BROILED TILAPIA

3 lbs. tilapia
1/4 C. oil
1/2 C. lemon juice
1/2 tsp. salt

1/2 tsp. pepper
1 T. oregano
1/4 tsp. garlic powder

Mix all ingredients except tilapia. Brush mixture over fish. Broil until golden brown. Place on serving platter and pour remaining mixture over tilapia.

## CHEESY STUFFED TILAPIA (DAIRY)

1 lb. tilapia
2 T. onion, chopped
1/4 C. ricotta cheese
1/4 C. broccoli, chopped

1 tsp. garlic powder
1/2 tsp. black pepper
2 T. butter, melted

Combine onion, ricotta cheese, broccoli and seasonings. Mix well. Divide mixture into 4 parts. Spread filling lengthwise on fish fillets. Fold fillets over filling, tucking fish under. Place the filled fish fillets, seam side down in a baking dish. Brush with melted margarine. Bake covered at 400°F for 30 minutes or until fish flakes apart easily when tested with a fork.

## TILAPIA IN LEMON DILL SAUCE

1 lb. tilapia fillets
3 T. vegetable broth (Imagine soup)
1 T. fresh dill, chopped or 3/4 tsp. dried dill

1 T. lemon juice
1/4 tsp. salt
1 medium scallion, finely sliced
Lemon slices for garnish

Heat broth and next 4 ingredients in a large skillet. Add tilapia to mixture in skillet, cover and cook 5-8 minutes until fish flakes easily when tested with fork. Garnish with lemon.

## FRESH WHITE FISH SALAD

1 lb. fresh white fish fillet
Lemon juice
Onion powder
Garlic powder

Salt
Tarragon
1 stalk celery
2 T. mayonnaise

Bake white fish in covered pan for 20 minutes at 350°F. Allow to cool. Separate skin from flesh. Mash the white fish flesh. Sprinkle with onion powder, garlic powder, tarragon, and salt. Dice celery and add to fish. Add mayonnaise and mix.

## FRESH QUINOA SALAD WITH SARDINES

1 1/2 C. cooked quinoa
1 tin sardine fillets, undrained
2 cucumbers, diced
1 large tomato, diced
1 small apple, unpeeled, diced

Juice of 1/2 lime
Salt, to taste
Ground cumin, to taste
Handful roasted pumpkin seeds, optional

Mix together all the ingredients. Taste to correct seasonings as needed. Serves 2. A delicious, high-protein quick lunch meal. Enjoy!


## POACHED FISH

1 lb. fish (salmon, tilapia, etc.)
1/2 C. water
Salt
Pepper

Lemon juice
Garlic powder
Dried Rosemary

Place fish in a baking pan. Add 1/2 C. water to pan. Sprinkle fish with seasonings, to taste. Bake at 350°F until fish juices run clear and form a white milky curd on top of fish (about 20 to 30 minutes, depending on thickness of fish).


## SAVORY PERCH

1 lb. Nile Perch fillets (or any other fresh fish)

1/2 C. mayonnaise
3 T. Dijon mustard

Place fillets in baking pan. Mix mayonnaise and mustard and spread over each fish fillet. Bake uncovered at 350°F until the fish is opaque and the top is golden brown. Kids love this recipe even though it's fish!

# Main Dishes

Main Dishes

# ROASTED CHICKEN AND VEGGIES

1 lb. small red potatoes,
    unpeeled and cut in half
2 carrots, cut in chunks
1 large onion, cut in wedges
12 garlic cloves, whole
2 T. olive oil
1 tsp. salt

3/4 tsp. dried rosemary
1/2 tsp. black pepper
2 lbs. chicken
1 red pepper, sliced
1 green pepper, sliced
1 C. hot water

Preheat oven to 425°F. Place potatoes, carrots, onion, garlic, and olive oil with 1/2 tsp. salt, 1/2 tsp. rosemary, and 1/4 tsp. black pepper in large ziploc bag and shake. Then place mixture in baking pan. Cover and bake for 20 minutes. Add chicken, peppers, hot water, 1/2 tsp. salt, 1/4 tsp. rosemary, and 1/4 tsp. black pepper. Bake covered for an hour. Uncover and bake for 10 minutes, or until crispy.

# APPLE CHICKEN

Chicken pieces
Dried apricots
Dried dates

Dried prunes
Unsweetened apple butter

Place chicken, apricots, dates, and prunes in a baking pan and add water to pan (about 1/4 inch deep). Coat chicken with apple butter. Cover pan and bake at 350F° for 2 hours. Uncover pan, raise heat to 425F° and bake for about 10 minutes, until crispy.

# CHICKEN TANDOORI

4 chicken quarters
1 large onion, diced
4 oz. can of sliced mushrooms
2 tsp. garlic powder

1 tsp. coriander
1 tsp. cumin
1 tsp. turmeric
1 tsp. chili powder

Place chicken, onion, and mushrooms in a baking pan, add a bit of water to pan (about 1/8" deep). Sprinkle with spices and cover. Bake for 2 hours at 350°F. Raise heat to 425°F, uncover and bake until crispy, about 10 minutes.

## OATMEAL CHICKEN CUTLETS

| | |
|---|---|
| 2 T. canola oil | 3/4 tsp. salt |
| 1 T. margarine, melted | 1 1/2 cups quick oats, uncooked |
| 2 tsp. chili powder | 1 egg, lightly beaten |
| 1 tsp. garlic powder | 1 T. water |
| 1 tsp. ground cumin | 4 chicken cutlets |

Heat oven to 375°F. Stir together oil, melted margarine, chili powder, garlic powder, cumin and salt. Add oats, stirring until evenly moistened.

In another bowl, beat egg and water with fork until frothy. Dip chicken into egg and water, then coat with seasoned oats. Place chicken on greased baking sheet. Bake 30 minutes or until chicken is cooked through and oat coating is golden brown.

## CRISPY CORNFLAKE CHICKEN

| | |
|---|---|
| 3 lb. chicken cutlets | 1/4 C. olive oil |
| 1/4 C. Dijon mustard | 1 1/2 tsp. Kosher salt |
| 6 C. unsweetened, gluten-free | 1 1/2 tsp. black pepper |
| cornflakes, crushed | |

Heat oven to 400°F. In a large ziploc bag, toss the chicken and mustard to coat. In a separate ziploc bag, crush the cornflakes, add olive oil, salt and pepper. Place chicken, one piece at a time, in bag with cornflake mixture and shake until coated. Bake chicken on a greased baking sheet until golden and cooked through, approximately 45 to 50 minutes.

## "BREADED" CHICKEN

| | |
|---|---|
| 1 C. oat bran | 1/2 tsp. salt |
| 2 T. paprika | 1/4 tsp. black pepper |
| 1 1/2 tsp. garlic powder | 4 chicken quarters |

Combine oat bran, paprika, garlic powder, salt, and pepper. Spray chicken all over with non-stick spray and dip into the oat bran mixture until covered. Bake in a single layer in a greased baking pan or cookie sheet on 350°F for approximately 1 hour, until cooked through.

## SUPER EASY ITALIAN CHICKEN

3 lb. chicken, cut in quarters          Jar of marinara sauce

Place chicken in pan and cover with marinara sauce. Cover pan and bake at 350°F for 2 hours. Uncover and bake at 425°F for 10 minutes, or until browned on top.
Variation: Add 1 cup of salsa in addition to marinara sauce to add some texture and spice.

## CHICKEN BALLS

2 lb. ground chicken                     1/8 tsp. black pepper
1 1/2 C. oat bran                        1 T. garlic powder
3 eggs, beaten                           1 T. onion powder
1 tsp. salt                              1 qt. chicken broth

Mix oat bran, eggs and spices. Add ground chicken. Mix well by hand and form into balls.
These can be served in soup instead of matza balls. Bring the soup to a boil and drop the balls into the boiling soup. Cover and simmer for 25 minutes.
Variation: Cook like regular meatballs - place in a pot with marinara sauce and simmer for one hour. Serve over brown rice.

## LEFTOVER CURRY CHICKEN

3 C. leftover chicken (great for          olive oil
    using up soup chicken)                1 T. curry
1 onion, chopped                          1/4 tsp. dry mustard or 1 tsp.
1 apple, diced                                regular mustard
1 red pepper, chopped                     1/4 tsp. dried parsley
2 stalks celery, chopped                  2 1/2 C. chicken or vegetable
4 cloves garlic, crushed                      broth (Imagine Soup is a good
                                              shortcut)

Sauté onions, apple, pepper, parsley, celery, and garlic in olive oil for 10 minutes or until soft. Add curry and mustard. Mix and sauté for 5 more minutes, stirring frequently. Add broth. Mix slowly until smooth. Cover and simmer for 1 hour. Mix with chicken pieces and serve with brown rice.

# LEFTOVER CHICKEN FRIED RICE

1/4 C. onion, diced
1/4 C. green pepper, diced
1/4 C. celery, diced
1 1/2 C. brown rice
1/2 C. green peas (fresh or frozen)

1 C. chicken, cooked and diced (great for using up leftover soup chicken)
2 eggs, beaten
1/4 C. bean sprouts
Soy Sauce

Bring 3 cups of water to a boil and add rice. Cover and simmer until water is absorbed, about 45 minutes.
Sauté onions, green pepper, and celery until tender. Remove from pan. Add more oil to pan, if necessary, and sauté rice. Add sautéed vegetables, peas, chicken and eggs. Sir for 2-3 minutes or until eggs are set but not dry or brown. Add bean sprouts. Season with soy sauce, to taste.

# LEFTOVER SPANISH CHICKEN

2 C. brown rice
1 T. oil
1 C. green peppers, diced
1 C. red peppers, diced
1/2 tsp. dried oregano
1/2 tsp. ground cumin

1 clove garlic, minced
2 C. chicken or vegetable broth or water
1 lb. cooked chicken, cut into 1/2-inch pieces (great for leftover soup chicken)
Salt and pepper

Heat oil in a large saucepan over medium heat. Add rice; sauté 10 minutes or until golden. Add onion, green peppers, red peppers, oregano, cumin and garlic; sauté 3 minutes. Add broth or water, salt, pepper, and chicken and bring to a boil. Cover, reduce heat, and simmer for 15 minutes or until liquid is absorbed.

# CHICKEN CACCIATORE

3 lbs. chicken, cut in eighths
1/2 C. onion, chopped
1/4 C. green pepper, chopped
1/2 C. celery, chopped
20 oz. canned tomatoes

1/2 tsp. salt
1 clove garlic, minced
1 tsp. parsley flakes
Dash of oregano

Brown pieces of chicken in skillet sprayed with nonstick vegetable cooking spray. Add remaining ingredients. Cover and simmer 1 hour.

# CHICKEN WITH ROASTED SWEET POTATO

2 sweet potatoes, peeled and cut into wedges
1 red onion, thinly sliced

3 T. olive oil
Salt and black pepper
1 1/2 lbs. chicken cutlets

Heat oven to 425°F. Toss the sweet potatoes, onion, 2 T. oil, 1/2 tsp. salt, and 1/4 tsp. pepper. Roast in a greased baking pan or cookie sheet until tender, about 20 to 25 minutes.
Heat the remaining tablespoon of oil in a skillet over medium-high heat. Season chicken with 1/2 tsp. salt and 1/4 tsp. pepper and cook until browned and cooked through, 5 to 6 minutes per side, depending upon thickness of cutlet. Serve sweet potato mixture with chicken.

# TOMATO BASIL CHICKEN

2 chickens, cut into eighths
4 garlic cloves, minced
2 large beefsteak tomatoes, diced
3 T. dried basil or 1/2 C. fresh basil

1/2 C. red wine vinegar
1/2 C. olive oil
1/4 tsp. black pepper
1 tsp. salt
5 sundried tomatoes

Preheat oven to 350°F. Place chicken in a single layer in two 9x13 pans. Process remaining ingredients in food processor with S-blade. Pour mixture over chicken and bake uncovered for 1 1/2 hours. Serve with brown rice.

## CHICKEN AND RICE RISOTTO

4 chicken cutlets, cut in small
   pieces
1 onion, diced
5 cloves garlic, minced
1 C. uncooked brown rice
1 T. olive oil

Water or chicken broth
1/2 tsp. turmeric
3/4 tsp. paprika
1 tsp. onion powder
1/2 tsp. salt
1/8 tsp. pepper

Place all ingredients in a large pot. Cover with water or broth to about a half inch above the ingredients. Bring to a boil, then lower heat to simmer. Cook for 1 1/2 to 2 hours, stirring once or twice, until the water is absorbed. Add more water if it gets too dry.

## CHICKEN DINNER IN A DISH

4 chicken quarters
2 potatoes, cut in chunks
2 carrots, cut in chunks
1 large onion, cut into wedges

1/2 C. chicken broth or water
1 bay leaf
Salt and pepper, to taste
8 oz. frozen green beans, thawed
   and drained

Heat oven to 350°F. Arrange chicken, potatoes, carrots and onion in baking dish. Pour broth over chicken; add bay leaf. Sprinkle with salt and pepper. Cover with foil. Bake at 350° for one hour.

Add green beans to chicken and vegetables. Turn oven up to 425°F, uncover pan, and bake for an additional 10-15 minutes or until chicken juices run clear and vegetables are tender. Remove bay leaf before serving.

## CHICKEN CHILI

2 medium onions, chopped
2 garlic cloves, minced
2 1/2 T. chili powder
2 tsp. ground cumin
1 tsp. dried oregano leaves
1/4 tsp. cayenne pepper
1 3/4 C. chicken broth or water
28 oz. can tomatoes, chopped, with juice
1 1/2 C. water

1 tsp. salt
1 bay leaf
2 lb. boneless, skinless chicken, cut into 1-inch chunks
2 medium zucchini, cut into cubes
16 oz. can black or white beans, rinsed and drained
11 oz. can unsweetened corn, drained

Sauté onions until just beginning to brown. Add garlic, chili powder, cumin, oregano and cayenne pepper. Sauté and stir for 1-2 minutes. Add chicken broth or water. Add tomatoes and juice, water, salt, chicken, zucchini, beans, corn, and bay leaf. Bring to a boil over high heat, reduce heat to low and simmer for 1 hour. Remove bay leaf.

## BEEF OR TURKEY CHILI WITH BEANS

2 lb. ground beef or turkey
1 green pepper, chopped
1 large onion, chopped
28 oz. canned tomatoes, chopped and drained
18 oz. can tomato paste

15 oz. can tomato puree
15 oz. can red kidney beans, drained
3 T. chili powder
2 tsp. salt
5 dashes Tabasco pepper sauce

Sauté meat, green pepper and onion in large skillet over medium heat until browned, stirring to crumble. Drain and put in crock pot. Add remaining ingredients. Cook overnight or all day. Instead of a crock pot, you can put all ingredients in a large pot, bring to a boil, reduce heat and simmer for 2 hours.

# BLACK BEAN CHILI

1 lb. dry black beans
2 large onions, chopped
1 C. bell peppers, chopped
3 cloves garlic, crushed
2 tsp. chili powder

2 tsp. cumin
2 tsp. dried cilantro
28 oz. can tomatoes, crushed
Salt and pepper, to taste

Soak beans according to package directions. Rinse. Place the beans, onion, peppers, garlic, chili powder, cumin and cilantro in 3 quarts of water. Bring to boil, then reduce to low heat. Simmer for about 2 hours, until beans are soft and water is gone. Add tomatoes. Cook until tomatoes are heated. Add salt and pepper to taste.

## BLACK AND RED CHILI

1 lb. ground beef
3 onions, diced
2 green peppers, chopped
3 T. chili powder
4 tsp. ground cumin
3 tsp. dried oregano
1/2 tsp. celery seed

3 - 8 oz. cans tomato sauce
2 - 15.5 oz. cans red beans, undrained
2 - 15.5 oz. cans black beans, undrained
2 - 14.5 oz. cans diced tomatoes, undrained

Sauté meat in large saucepan over medium heat until browned, stirring to crumble. Add onion and pepper; sauté 3 minutes. Add remaining ingredients. Bring to a boil. Reduce heat and simmer, uncovered for 30 minutes, stirring occasionally.

## 10 MINUTE CHILI

2 - 15.5 oz. cans red kidney
    beans, undrained
14.5 oz. can tomatoes, crushed,
    diced or chopped, undrained
8 oz. tomato sauce
6 oz. tomato paste
1 large onion, diced
1 lb. ground beef

2 cloves garlic, chopped
1/4 tsp. salt
1/4 tsp. black pepper
2 T. chili powder
1 tsp. cumin powder
6 oz. water (more for thinner or
    less for thicker)

Brown crumbled ground beef and onion. Stir in the rest of the ingredients. Simmer for 10 minutes.

# KASHA CHILI

28-oz. can stewed tomatoes
3 C. vegetable broth (Imagine soup)
1 can pinto beans
1 T. chili powder
1 tsp. paprika

1 tsp. minced garlic
1 tsp. ground cumin
1 tsp. dried oregano
1/2 tsp. celery salt, optional
1/4 tsp. black pepper
3/4 C. whole dry kasha

In a large skillet, combine all ingredients except kasha. Bring to a light boil for 10 minutes. Add kasha, cover, and reduce to simmer. Simmer for 10 to 15 minutes, or until kasha is tender.

# QUICK CHILI

1/2 C. dry textured vegetable protein (TVP)
1/2 C. boiling water
1 onion, chopped
1 green pepper, diced
2 garlic cloves, minced
1/2 C. water or vegetable broth (Imagine Soup)

2 - 15 oz. cans pinto beans
15 oz. can tomato sauce
1 C. frozen corn
2 tsp. chili powder
1 tsp. dried oregano
1/2 tsp. ground cumin
1/8 tsp. cayenne pepper, or to taste

Pour the boiling water over textured vegetable protein and let stand until softened. Sauté onion, bell pepper, and garlic until onion is soft. Add broth or water, beans, tomato sauce, corn, chili powder, oregano, cumin, cayenne, and textured vegetable protein. Simmer for 30 minutes.

# SWEET AND SOUR MEATBALLS

2 lb. ground beef or chicken
1/2 C. pureed vegetables (you can use baby food jars of carrots, squash, sweet potatoes, peas, green beans)

1 C. natural fruit spread (no sugar or Splenda added)
14 oz. jar marinara sauce

Roll the meat into balls and place in a baking pan. Combine the remaining ingredients and pour over the meatballs. Cover and bake for 1 hour at 350°F.

## EASY ITALIAN MEATBALLS

Large jar of marinara sauce          1 lb. chopped beef or turkey

Shape meat into small balls and place in pot. Pour marinara sauce over meatballs. Bring to a soft boil, cover and simmer for 1 hour.


## MEATLOAF

1 lb. ground beef                     1 1/2 tsp. salt
1 lb. ground turkey or chicken        1/4 tsp. black pepper
3/4 C. oat bran                       Dash thyme
2 eggs                                Dash marjoram
16 oz. can tomato sauce               Dash onion powder
1/2 C. onion, chopped or dash
  of onion powder

Preheat oven to 350°F. Combine all ingredients and mix well. Pat into a greased baking pan. Bake for one hour.


## EASY ROAST BEEF

3 lb. boneless beef roast             Garlic powder
4 bay leaves                          Paprika
Soy sauce

Sprinkle meat with soy sauce, garlic powder, and paprika. Lay bay leaves on top. Add water to bottom of pan, about 1/8". Bake covered at 350°F until tender, at least 1 hour. Remove bay leaves before serving.

## MINUTE STEAK

1 lb. minute steaks
2 sweet onions, diced
1 package or can mushrooms,
  sliced

Salt and pepper, to taste
Garlic powder

Sauté onion until golden, add mushrooms and sauté for a few more minutes. Place minute steaks on top of the onions and mushrooms. Sprinkle with salt, pepper, and garlic powder. Cover and simmer for 10 minutes. Flip steaks, add some more seasonings and cover and simmer for another 10 minutes. Serve with kasha.

## SMOTHERED STEAK

1 lb. steak
1 tsp. garlic powder
1 C. bell pepper, chopped

1 C. onions, chopped
1 large tomato, sliced thin

In large pan, fry steaks on both sides until brown. Add garlic powder, pepper, and onions. Cover pan and simmer for 5 minutes. Garnish with tomato slices.

## EASY POT ROAST

3 lb. beef roast
1 1/2 C. water
1 tsp. black pepper
2 onions, chopped
2 bay leaves
1 C. canned, undrained crushed
  tomatoes

4 carrots, diced
4 stalks celery, diced
2 turnips, diced
4 T. fresh parsley or 4 tsp. dried
  parsley
1/2 tsp. dried thyme

Place all ingredients in a large baking dish and cover. Cook at 350°F for 3 hours.

# YANKEE POT ROAST

2 lb. beef roast
3 C. tomato juice
2 C. onion, thinly sliced
2 garlic cloves, minced
1/4 tsp. black pepper
1/4 tsp. salt

1 tsp. basil
1 tsp. thyme
1/4 C. dried marjoram
1/2 C. mushrooms, sliced
2 tsp. dried parsley

Preheat oven to 325°F. Combine onion, tomato juice and spices. Place roast in a baking pan, cover with onion mixture, cover and bake for 3 hours or until tender.
Sauté mushrooms and stir until brown. Remove roast, slice and place on a platter. Mix mushrooms with onion mixture and pour over meat. Sprinkle with parsley and serve.

# NEW ENGLAND CORNED BEEF

4 lbs. corned beef brisket
5 onions, sliced
4 turnips, sliced
6 potatoes, cut in chunks
6 carrots, cut in chunks

1 lb. cabbage, cut in quarters
Mustard Sauce (optional)
1/3 C. prepared mustard
1 T. prepared white horseradish
  sauce

Place corned beef in 6-1/2 quart Dutch oven; cover with 1" of water. Bring to a boil; reduce heat and simmer for 2 1/2 to 3 hours or until almost tender. Add onions and turnips; cook for 30 minutes. Add potatoes, carrots and cabbage. Cook for 20 minutes or until meat and vegetables are tender. Combine mustard and horseradish and serve with beef and vegetables, if desired.

## BEEF AND BEET STEW

1 large onion, diced
2 large beets, peeled and
  cubed
1 lb. beef cubes
28 oz. can crushed tomatoes

Salt
Pepper
1 tsp. dried rosemary
1 T. garlic, chopped
1 lemon, sliced

Sauté onions on medium high heat until onions are slightly brown and caramelized. Add garlic and sauté for 2 more minutes. Add salt, pepper and beef. Sauté for 3 more minutes. Add remaining ingredients and simmer for several hours or put into crock pot and leave overnight. Serve with quinoa or brown rice.

## SWEET POTATO SHEPHERD'S PIE

I lb. ground beef
2 T. tomato sauce
I tsp. dried basil
Small onion, finely grated
I tsp. black pepper

I egg, beaten
Topping:
4 sweet potatoes
1 egg

Preheat oven to 350ºF. Combine all the ingredients for the meat mixture and mix well. Press into a greased baking dish. Cover and bake for 30 minutes.
Bake sweet potatoes for 1 hour. Peel and mix well with egg.
When meat is done, pour gravy from pan into the sweet potatoes and mix. Spread sweet potatoes over the meat. Cover and bake at 350ºF for 15 minutes, then raise oven to 425ºF, uncover and bake for 10 more minutes.

# CHOLENT

1-2 lbs. beef kalky or beef cubes
4 potatoes, white or sweet or
   combination of both
1/4 C. brown rice, barley, or
   quinoa
1 onion, chopped
1/2 C. beans, rinsed

3 cloves garlic, minced
1 tsp. paprika
Dash of curry powder
1 tsp. cumin
Dash of chili powder
1 tsp. salt
Dash of black pepper

Mix ingredients in crock pot, cover with water (about 1" above ingredients), and turn crock pot to high setting. When it comes to a boil, turn heat to low.

# CROCK POT GOULASH

1 lb. of beef cubes
2 onions, sliced
4 potatoes, cut in chunks
2 carrots, sliced
1 zucchini, cut in chunks
15 oz. can tomato sauce

1 T. olive oil
Garlic powder
Paprika
Black pepper
Salt

Place all ingredients in crock pot on high heat. Bring to a boil and then lower heat to simmer.

## MOROCCAN VEGETABLE STEW

1 medium onion, diced
1/2 tsp. coriander
1/4 tsp. turmeric
1/2 tsp. cinnamon
1/2 tsp. ginger
1/4 tsp. cumin
2 medium tomatoes, chopped
1 sweet potato, peeled and
   chopped

1/4 C. water
2 T. lemon juice
15 oz. can chickpeas, drained
   and rinsed
1 small zucchini, cut into chunks
3 T. parsley
1/4 C. raisins

Sauté onion and spices for about 10 minutes, stirring frequently. Add tomatoes, sweet potato, water, and lemon juice. Bring to a boil, reduce heat, cover, and simmer for 30 minutes. Add chickpeas, zucchini, parsley, and raisins. Simmer for another 10 minutes.

## MEXICAN TURKEY BURGERS

1 lb. ground turkey
1 T. chili powder

2 T. minced garlic
Black pepper, to taste

Mix all ingredients together and form into 4 patties. Broil or grill approximately 7 minutes on each side or until done. They can also be cooked in a medium skillet over medium heat for about 5 minutes. Flip the burgers and cook for another 5 minutes, or until inside is no longer pink.

## SPICY TURKEY LOAF

2 lbs. ground turkey
10 oz. frozen chopped spinach,
   thawed and drained
1/2 C. onion, finely chopped
1/2 C. bell pepper, chopped
1/2 C. carrots, shredded
4 egg whites, beaten
2 T. water

2 tsp. cumin
2 tsp. oregano
1 tsp. thyme
1 tsp. paprika
1 tsp. salt
1/8 tsp. crushed red pepper
   flakes

Preheat oven to 350°F. Mix all ingredients well and place in greased baking pan. Bake for 1 hour.

## TURKEY LOAF

1 lb. ground turkey
1/2 C. oat bran
1 egg

2 tsp. salt
1/4 tsp. black pepper
1/4 tsp. tarragon

Mix ingredients and place in greased baking pan. Bake covered at 400°F for 35 minutes.


## APPLE TURKEY PATTIES

2 tsp. vegetable oil
1 onion, finely chopped
2 C. Granny Smith apples, grated
1 lb. ground turkey
1 C. oat bran
2 egg whites

2 tsp. dried sage
1 1/2 tsp. salt
1/4 tsp. black pepper
1/4 tsp. nutmeg
1/4 tsp. allspice

Mix all ingredients and form into patties. Bake patties in greased baking pan at 350°F for 30 minutes, turning once.

# RED BEAN CASSEROLE

3 C. cooked brown rice
2 - 15-oz. cans red beans,
   drained and rinsed
1 C. red onion, chopped
1 garlic clove, minced

1 C. celery, chopped
1 T. dried parsley
1 tsp. salt
1/2 tsp. black pepper
Dash of chili pepper

Preheat oven to 350°F. Combine ingredients and place in a greased baking pan. Bake uncovered for 20 minutes.

# CHICKPEAS IN TOMATO SAUCE

1 medium onion, chopped
2 T. olive oil
1 C. tomatoes, chopped
1 bay leaf
2 garlic cloves, minced
16 oz. can chickpeas, drained

1 tsp. salt
Black pepper, to taste
1 tsp. cumin
1/2 tsp. turmeric
1/2 C. water

Sauté onion in olive oil. Add tomatoes, bay leaf, garlic, and chickpeas and stir. Add water, salt, pepper, cumin and turmeric. Cover and cook over medium heat for 15 minutes. Remove bay leaf and serve over cooked grain.

# "STUFFED" CABBAGE

3 C. cabbage, shredded
1 lb. ground beef
1/2 tsp. oregano
1 1/4 tsp. garlic powder or 2
   cloves garlic, minced
1 1/4 tsp. dried parsley
Dash of dried ginger

Dash of dried mustard
1 C. celery, chopped
1 C. onion, chopped
1 C. green pepper, chopped
1 small can crushed tomatoes
1 tsp. dried basil

Cook the cabbage in the microwave or in a steamer until tender. Sauté ground beef, spices, celery, onion, and green pepper until meat is browned. Add the crushed tomatoes. Serve the meat mixture over a bed of cabbage and garnish with basil.

# SHAKSHUKA

2 medium onions, diced          20 oz. tomato sauce
1 T. oil                        10 eggs
2 tomatoes, diced

Sauté onions for 5 minutes on medium heat. Add tomatoes and sauté for 2 more minutes. Add tomato sauce. Crack the eggs carefully and pour over the tomato sauce, keeping them whole. Cover the pan and cook on medium heat for 10 minutes, or until the eggs are done.

# TEMPEH BROCCOLI STIR FRY

10 oz. tempeh                   1 red bell pepper, diced
1/4 C. vegetable broth (Imagine 1 T. garlic, minced
  soup)                         1 tsp. ground ginger
32 oz. frozen broccoli florets  1 T. soy sauce
1 small onion, diced

Cut tempeh into small cubes and steam for 10 minutes or heat in microwave. Heat the broth in a large pan and add the tempeh, broccoli, onion, bell pepper, garlic, and ginger. Cook on medium-high heat, stirring frequently, until the tempeh is lightly browned and the vegetables are tender, about 7 minutes. Add the soy sauce just before serving.

# CRUNCHY TOFU STICKS

1 lb. extra firm tofu, drained
3 T. soy sauce
1 T. rice vinegar
1 clove garlic, crushed
5 T. unsweetened soy milk
1/2 tsp. olive oil
1 C. unsweetened gluten-free
   cornflakes, mashed

1 tsp. garlic powder
1 tsp. paprika
2 tsp. dried parsley
salt and pepper, to taste
2 T. sesame seeds

Preheat oven to 400°F. Cut tofu into thin, long sticks.
Mix soy sauce, rice vinegar and crushed garlic. Pour over tofu and marinate for 30 minutes.
Mix the soy milk and oil. In a separate bowl, mix the cornflake crumbs, spices and sesame seeds. Carefully dip the tofu sticks in the soy milk and oil mixture, then coat with the cornflake crumb mixture. Lay tofu sticks on a greased baking sheet. Bake 30 minutes, turning the sticks once to evenly brown.

# LAMB STUFFED EGGPLANT

1 small eggplant
1 C. onion, chopped
1 C. red pepper, chopped
1 C. tomato, chopped
2 cloves garlic, chopped
10 oz. ground lamb

2/3 C. Old-Fashioned oats
Salt, to taste
1/2 tsp. black pepper
1 tsp. cinnamon
1 T. dried basil
1 T. Cumin

Cut the eggplants in half lengthwise and scoop out the center, leaving 1/2-inch of "meat" inside the skin so that it holds its shape when baked.
Sauté onion, pepper, tomato, and garlic in olive oil until onions are transparent. Add lamb and cook until lamb is browned.
Mix chopped eggplant, sautéed vegetables, lamb, oatmeal and spices. Place into eggplant skins and bake at 400°F for 30 minutes.

## BEEF STUFFED EGGPLANT

2 eggplants
1 medium onion, chopped
1 clove garlic, minced
2 T. oil

1/2 lb. ground beef
2 C. tomatoes, fresh or canned
Salt, to taste
1/2 tsp. basil

Preheat oven to 350°F. Cut the eggplants in half lengthwise and scoop out the center, leaving 1/2-inch of "meat" inside the skin so that it holds its shape when baked.
Dice eggplant pulp. Sauté onion, garlic and eggplant pulp in oil. Add ground beef, tomatoes, salt, and basil. Fill eggplant shells with mixture.
Place filled eggplant halves in greased baking pan and bake at 350°F for 50 minutes.


## ITALIAN VEAL AND PEPPERS

2 medium onions, chopped
2 lb. veal cutlets

4 green peppers, sliced in strips
1 jar of marinara sauce

Sauté onions until golden brown. Add veal and peppers and cook for 10 minutes on medium heat. Stir in marinara sauce. Simmer, covered 45 minutes.

# Side Dishes

## ZUCCHINI SWEET POTATO LATKES

2 medium potatoes, shredded
1 small zucchini, shredded and
  drained
1 small sweet potato, shredded
1 small onion, grated

2 eggs, beaten
1 1/4 tsp. salt
6 T. oat bran
3 T. olive oil

Mix all the ingredients (except the oil) in a large bowl. Heat 3 T. olive oil in a frying pan at medium-high heat. Place spoonfuls of mixture into pan and flatten each with spatula. Fry latkes until golden brown on both sides.

## SPICY POTATO LATKES

2 lbs. Yukon Gold potatoes,
  shredded and drained
1 small onion, grated
1 tsp. chili pepper flakes or 1T.
  fresh jalapeno pepper, minced

3 eggs, beaten
2 tsp. salt
2 tsp. chili powder
1/2 C. oat bran
Olive oil for frying

Mix all ingredients (except the oil). Heat 3 T. olive oil in a frying pan at a medium-high heat. Place heaping spoonfuls of mixture into pan. Fry latkes until golden brown onto both sides, adding more oil as necessary.

## POTATO LATKES

6 medium potatoes, grated
1 onion, grated
2 eggs, well-beaten

3 T. oat bran
Salt and pepper, to taste

Mix all ingredients well. Coat skillet with vegetable spray or olive oil and drop mixture by spoonfuls into pan. Brown well on both sides.

# POTATO-BEET LATKES

3 T. olive oil
1 small onion, pureed
2 eggs, beaten
3 potatoes, shredded
2 medium beets, boiled or
microwaved, drained and
shredded

1/2 C. ground walnuts
1/2 C. oat bran
1 tsp. salt
1/4 tsp. pepper

Mix all ingredients well. Heat olive oil in a pan. Drop mixture by spoonfuls into pan. Brown well on both sides.

# BAKED LATKES

4 tsp. olive oil
2 lbs. potatoes
1 medium onion
1 clove garlic
1 T. fresh dill or 1 tsp. dried dill

2 eggs
1/2 tsp. baking powder
3/4 tsp. salt
1/4 tsp. pepper

Place oven racks on the lowest and middle positions. Preheat oven to 450°F. In food processor, finely mince onion, garlic and dill, using S-blade. Then add potatoes, eggs, and 2 tsp. of oil. Add remaining ingredients and mix briefly. Drop mixture by spoonfuls onto greased cookie sheet. Flatten latkes slightly and spray them with non-stick spray. Bake uncovered for 10 minutes, or until bottoms are nicely browned and crispy. Flip latkes. Bake about 8 to 10 minutes longer, or until brown.

# POTATO KUGEL

12 large potatoes, grated
8 eggs, beaten

1/2 C. oil
2 T. salt

Preheat oven to 400°F. Pour the oil into a baking pan and heat in oven. Mix potatoes, eggs, and salt. Wearing oven mitts, very carefully pour mixture into pan with heated oil, making sure that it doesn't splatter on you. Bake for 1 hour or until brown and crispy.

## VEGETABLE BARLEY KUGEL

1 C. barley
1 large onion, chopped
1 C. mushrooms, chopped
1 lb. zucchini, shredded
2 large carrots, shredded

2 eggs, beaten
1/2 tsp. thyme
1 tsp. dill
1 tsp. lemon juice

Place barley in 3 C. boiling water, cover and simmer until water is absorbed.
Sauté onions, carrots, zucchini and mushrooms until onions are soft.
Stir vegetables and barley together. Add eggs, lemon juice, thyme and dill and mix thoroughly. Place mixture in greased baking pan and cover. Bake for 40 minutes at 350°F, uncover and bake 30 minutes more or until brown and pulls away from the side.


## BROCCOLI POTATO KUGEL

4 potatoes, shredded
4 carrots, shredded
2 lb. frozen chopped broccoli,
    thawed and drained

5 eggs
3/4 C. mayonnaise
2 T. onion flakes
1 T. salt

Beat eggs. Add mayonnaise, salt, and onion flakes. Add all vegetables to beaten egg mixture and pour into greased baking dish. Bake at 350°F uncovered for about 45 minutes.


## LEMON RED POTATOES

2 lbs. small red potatoes, halved
3 T. lemon juice
3 T. olive oil

2 tsp. salt
1/2 tsp. ground pepper
3 T. dried parsley

Preheat oven to 375°F. Place potatoes in a baking pan. Combine the remaining ingredients, and pour over the potatoes. Bake for 1 hour. Sprinkle with parsley before serving.

## BAKED FRENCH FRIES

2 lbs. potatoes
4 T. olive oil

Salt
Pepper

Preheat oven to 400°F. Peel and slice potatoes into French fry wedges. Wrap slices in a paper towel to remove any excess moisture. Place potatoes, olive oil, salt and pepper into a ziploc bag and shake. Spread potatoes in a single layer on a greased baking sheet and bake for 10 minutes. Flip the potatoes and bake for another 10 to 15 minutes.


## ROASTED POTATOES AND VEGETABLES

4 large potatoes, cut in large
  chunks
1 red onion, cut in wedges
3 T. vegetable oil
1 1/2 tsp. salt
2 bags baby carrots
1/2 lb. yellow squash, cut into
  bite-sized chunks

1/2 lb. green beans, stems
  trimmed
2 red peppers, cut into chunks
2 yellow peppers, cut into chunks
1 tsp. dried thyme
1/2 tsp. black pepper
1/2 lemon, sliced

Preheat oven to 425°F. In a large baking pan, toss potatoes and onion with 1 T. vegetable oil and 1/2 tsp. salt. Bake for 15 minutes. Add remaining ingredients. Bake for 45 minutes.


## PESTO POTATOES

2 lbs. potatoes, cubed
1/3 C. olive oil
2 T. pine nuts

1/4 C. basil
2 cloves garlic
Salt and black pepper, to taste

Place potatoes in a greased baking pan and spray with nonstick spray. Bake at 425°F for 1 hour. Mix remaining ingredients in a food processor or blender. Pour sauce over potatoes and serve.

## DIJON RED POTATO WEDGES

6 T. Dijon mustard
3 T. oil
2 cloves garlic, crushed
1 T. lemon juice

1 tsp. parsley flakes
1/2 tsp. salt
1/4 tsp. black pepper
3 lb. small red potatoes, cut into
    wedges

Preheat oven to 425°F. Mix mustard, oil, garlic, lemon juice, parsley, salt and pepper. Add potatoes and mix well. Spread potatoes in a single layer on greased baking sheet. Bake 45 minutes.

## MASHED POTATOES

4 lbs. Yukon Gold potatoes,
    peeled
1/2 C. margarine

2 C. unsweetened soy milk
2 tsp. salt
1 tsp. black pepper

Bring potatoes to a boil, reduce heat, and simmer 10 minutes or until tender. Drain. Place all ingredients in a bowl and whip with a mixer or immersion blender. Add additional salt and pepper to taste.

## CRUNCHY POTATO FRIES

2 lbs. baking potatoes
1 egg white
1/2 tsp. salt

1/4 tsp. pepper
1/4 C. cornflake crumbs

Preheat oven to 450°F. Grease a baking sheet and set aside. Cut potatoes into strips. In a shallow medium bowl, beat egg white. Stir in salt and pepper. Dip potatoes strips into egg white mixture then place on prepared baking sheet. Sprinkle each strip with cornflake crumbs. Bake in preheated oven for 20 to 25 minutes, until potatoes are crisp and golden. Serve warm. Makes 4 servings.

## COUNTRY FRIES WITH CARROTS

1/2 red onion, diced
2 C. carrots, diced
3 T. oil
1/2 C. water
1 lb. potatoes, diced in very
    small pieces

Dash of ginger
2 tsp. curry
1 1/2 tsp. salt
1 1/2 tsp. black pepper

Heat oil in skillet on medium heat. Sauté onion and carrots on medium heat for 5 minutes. Add potatoes, ginger, curry, salt, pepper and water. Cover and cook for 30 minutes, or until liquid is absorbed.


## BAKED SWEET POTATO CHIPS

Sweet potatoes, sliced very thin
Cinnamon

Cooking oil spray

Preheat oven to 400°F. Slice sweet potatoes very thin, or use food processor with slicing blade. Spray baking pan with cooking oil and lay sweet potatoes in a single layer on pan. Spray sweet potatoes and sprinkle with cinnamon. Bake until brown around edges, about 15 minutes.


## SWEET POTATO KUGEL

6 small sweet potatoes, peeled
    and grated
3 apples, peeled and grated
1 C. raisins

1 C. ground almonds
2 tsp. cinnamon
1 C. fruit juice or water

Preheat oven to 375°F. Mix ingredients together. Press into greased baking pan. Bake 45 minutes, or until crisp on top.

## CRISPY SWEET POTATOES

4 medium sweet potatoes      1/4 tsp. salt
1 egg white

Preheat oven to 425°F. Scrub and cut sweet potatoes into quarters. Dip quarters into egg whites and place on greased baking pan. Bake for 20-25 minutes or until soft when pierced with a fork. Turn potatoes once during baking. Serve immediately.


## FRUITY TZIMMES

2 medium onions
3 medium sweet potatoes
1 medium butternut squash
1 lb. parsnips
2 lb. carrots
4 apples
1 C. orange juice

1/2 tsp. dried coriander
2 tsp. cinnamon
1/2 tsp. ground cloves
1/2 C. prunes
1/4 C. dried dates
1/4 C. dried apricots

Peel and chop vegetables and apples. Combine orange juice and spices. Pour juice over vegetables and fruit in a big pot; add enough water to cover 1/3 of the vegetables. Bring to a boil, then cover and simmer for 1 hour. Mash mixture.


## BAKED TZIMMES

3 sweet potatoes, peeled and
    cut into chunks
12 carrots, peeled and cut into
    chunks
1/2 C. dried apricots
1/2 C. pitted prunes

1/2 C. orange juice or more, as
    needed
3 T. margarine
1/2 tsp. cinnamon
1/8 tsp. salt

Preheat oven to 375°F. Combine potatoes, carrots, fruit, and margarine in greased baking pan. Pour orange juice over mixture to cover the bottom with 1/4 inch of juice. Cover and bake for 1 hour. Uncover and bake an additional 10 minutes.

# QUINOA PILAF

| | |
|---|---|
| 1 yellow or red onion, chopped | 2 C. quinoa |
| 1/2 C. celery, chopped | 1 tsp. salt |
| 1/2 C. carrot, chopped | 4 C. boiling water or vegetable broth |
| 1 garlic clove, minced | |
| 2 tsp. ground cumin | 1/4 C. fresh cilantro or parsley, minced or 4 T. dried cilantro or parsley |
| 1 tsp. dried oregano | |

Sauté onion, celery, carrot, and garlic until they start to turn brown. Add cumin, oregano, salt, and quinoa. Stir constantly and cook for about 3 more minutes to allow spices and quinoa to toast. Add boiling water or vegetable broth. Cover and cook about 20 minutes or until all the liquid has completely absorbed. Add cilantro or parsley. Fluff with a fork and serve.

## QUINOA WITH NUTS AND DRIED FRUIT

| | |
|---|---|
| 1 C. quinoa | 1/2 C. walnuts and/or almonds |
| 2 C. water | 1/2 C. dried fruit cut into small pieces (dried apricots, peaches and raisins work well) |
| 1/2 tsp. salt | |
| Cinnamon to taste | |

Heat large skillet on high heat. Place uncooked quinoa in pan and stir constantly for a couple of minutes to toast it. Bring water and salt to a boil and then place toasted quinoa into water. Simmer, covered, for 15 minutes. Add remaining ingredients and mix well.

## GARLIC QUINOA

| | |
|---|---|
| 1 C. quinoa | 6 cloves of garlic, minced |
| 2 C. water or broth | 1/2 tsp. salt |
| 1/2 onion, chopped | |

Sauté garlic and onions in olive oil.
Heat large skillet on high heat. Place uncooked quinoa in pan and stir constantly for a couple of minutes to toast it.
Bring water and salt to a boil and then place toasted quinoa into water. Simmer, covered, for 15 minutes. Combine quinoa and onions and garlic and toss well.

## QUINOA TABOULEH

2 C. quinoa
4 C. water
1 C. fresh parsley, chopped or
   1/3 C. dried parsley
3 green onions (scallions),
   chopped

1 C. plum tomatoes, chopped
1 garlic clove, minced
1/4 C. olive oil
Juice of one lemon
Salt, to taste

Heat large skillet on high heat. Place uncooked quinoa in pan and stir constantly for a couple of minutes to toast it. Bring water and salt to a boil and then place toasted quinoa into water. Cover and cook about 20 minutes or until all the liquid has completely absorbed.
Combine cooked quinoa with parsley, onions and tomatoes. Whisk garlic, olive oil, lemon juice and salt together. Mix well with quinoa mixture.

## BROWN RICE STUFFING

2 tsp. margarine
2 apples, diced
1/2 C. onion, chopped
1/2 C. celery, chopped
1/2 tsp. sage
1/4 tsp. marjoram

1/4 tsp. rosemary
1/4 tsp. dried thyme
1/4 tsp. ground white pepper
3 C. brown rice
3 C. water and 3 C. chicken
   broth (or just 6 C. water)

Bring water and broth (or just water) to a boil. Add rice, cover, and simmer on low heat for 45 minutes or until all the water is absorbed. Sauté apples, onion, celery and seasonings in margarine until tender. Stir in cooked rice; continue cooking until heated through. Stuff into whole turkey or serve as a side dish with poultry.

## BROWN RICE PILAF

| | |
|---|---|
| 1/2 C. celery, chopped | 1/4 tsp. marjoram |
| 1/2 C. onion, chopped | 1/4 tsp. rosemary |
| 1/2 C. green pepper, chopped | 1 C. raw brown rice |
| 1/2 C. carrots, chopped | 2 C. vegetable broth (Imagine |
| 1 clove garlic | Soup) or water |
| 1/4 tsp. paprika | 1/2 tsp. salt |
| 1/4 tsp. sage | |

Sauté vegetables until onions are golden and celery is tender - about 20 minutes. Sir in herbs and uncooked rice. Add broth or water to rice mixture and bring to a boil. Lower heat, cover and simmer until all the liquid is absorbed and rice is tender, about 45 minutes.

## ALMOND RICE

| | |
|---|---|
| 1 C. chicken or vegetable broth | 1/8 tsp. saffron |
| 2 C. water | 1/8 tsp. salt |
| 1 C. brown rice | Pepper to taste |
| 2 T. slivered almonds | |

In a medium saucepan over high heat, bring chicken broth and water to a boil. Stir in rice, slivered almonds, saffron and salt. Add pepper to taste and return to a boil. Immediately reduce heat to low. Cover saucepan and simmer for 45 minutes, until rice is tender and all liquid has absorbed.

## MEXICAN RICE

| | |
|---|---|
| 1 clove garlic | 4 T. oil |
| 1/4 medium onion | 1 C. raw brown rice |
| 4 plum tomatoes | 1 tsp. salt |
| 1 C. water | |

In food processor, blend garlic, onion, tomatoes and water. Sauté rice in oil, stirring constantly for 5 minutes. Drain most of oil out. Add tomato mixture to rice. Cook for 5 minutes over high flame. Lower flame, cover pot and cook for 20 to 25 minutes.

## SPICY RICE AND CHICKPEAS

2 C. water
1/2 tsp. salt
1/8 tsp. crushed red pepper
   flakes
1 C. brown rice
1 T. olive oil

1 garlic clove, minced
1 carrot, shredded
1 can chickpeas, drained
1 tsp. ground ginger
3 T. lemon juice

Bring water, salt, and pepper flakes to a boil. Add rice, cover, and simmer until water is absorbed, about 45 minutes.
Sauté garlic and carrots for 5 minutes. Add chickpeas, ginger, and lemon juice. Stir well until all ingredients are heated. Serve chickpea mixture over rice.


## RICE AND BARLEY PILAF

1 C. onion, minced
1 C. brown rice
1/2 C. barley
2 garlic cloves, minced
3 1/2 C. water or broth
1 C. fresh mushrooms, sliced

1 C. celery, thinly sliced
1 C. carrots, thinly sliced
1/2 C. fresh parsley, chopped or
  2 T. dried parsley
1 T. soy sauce

Heat 1 tablespoon oil in large saucepan over medium heat. Add onion; cook and stir about 10 minutes or until tender. Add barley, rice and garlic; cook and stir over medium heat 1 minute.
Stir in 3 1/2 C. water or broth. Bring to a boil over medium-high heat. Reduce heat to low; simmer, covered, about 1 hour or until barley and rice are tender.
Heat remaining 1 tablespoon oil in large skillet over medium-high heat. Add mushrooms, celery, carrot and parsley; cook and stir 5 to 10 minutes or until vegetables are tender.
Stir vegetable mixture into rice and barley mixture.

## SUMMER BARLEY MEDLEY

1 C. barley
6 yellow squash, sliced
2 onions, diced
2 C. corn, frozen or canned,
    unsweetened

1 tsp. ground thyme
Salt and pepper, to taste
Parsley

Place barley in 3 C. boiling water, cover and simmer until water is absorbed. Sauté squash and onion. Combine barley with squash mixture and remaining ingredients. Garnish with parsley.

## MILLET WITH CAULIFLOWER

2 C. millet
4 C. cauliflower florets, frozen
2 onions, diced

6 C. boiling water
Sesame oil
1 tsp. salt

Sauté onions in sesame oil until golden brown. Add boiling water and salt. Add millet, cover and reduce heat. Simmer for 30 minutes, until water is almost completely absorbed. Add cauliflower and simmer for 5 more minutes.

# Desserts

# &

# Smoothies

# NUT-FILLED PEARS

4 pears
3 T. nuts, chopped

1 tsp. cinnamon
1/2 C. orange juice

Core the pears. Mix nuts and cinnamon. Fill each pear cavity with nuts and cinnamon. Place pears in a baking pan and pour orange juice over the pears. Bake at 350°F for 20 minutes. Serve warm.

# BAKED APPLES

4 large apples, cored
Vegetable oil
1 T. cinnamon
1/2 C. shredded unsweetened
   coconut

1/2 C. ground nuts
3/4 C. water or orange juice

Preheat oven to 400°F. Mix cinnamon, coconut, and nuts. Coat apples with oil, then roll in coconut mixture. Place apples in a baking pan. Stuff each apple with any remaining mixture. Add water or orange juice to the baking pan. Bake at 400° for at least 1 hour, until very soft inside.

# BAKED FRUIT DELIGHT

2 medium apples, unpeeled, cut
   into chunks
8 oz. can pineapple chunks in its
   own juice
1/2 C. grapes

1 orange, peeled and sectioned
1/2 C. orange juice
1 T. vegetable oil
1/4 tsp. ground cinnamon

Preheat oven to 350°F. In a baking dish, combine apples, pineapple, grapes, and orange. Drizzle with orange juice and oil and sprinkle with cinnamon. Cover and bake until the apples are tender, about 30 minutes.

## SUMMER FRUIT COMPOTE

2 C. fresh or frozen peaches,
   sliced

2 C. strawberries
1/4 C. apple juice concentrate*

Combine ingredients in a large saucepan. Bring to a simmer and cook for about 5 minutes, or until the fruit just becomes soft.
* Apple juice concentrate is a sweetener and should not be used by those who are abstaining from sweeteners.


## GRILLED PINEAPPLE

1 pineapple, peeled and
   chopped into chunks
Allspice, lightly sprinkled
Ground ginger, generous
   sprinkling

Salt, couple of pinches
Coconut spray (optional)
Nonstick spray

Preheat oven to 450°F. Spray pan with nonstick spray and place pineapple in single layer. Add seasonings, spray pineapple with both sprays. Bake for a few minutes, until soft and edges start to brown.


## CHUNKY APPLE DELIGHT

4 apples, cubed in large chunks
1 1/2 tsp. cinnamon
Ginger, generous sprinkling

Ground coriander seed, light
   sprinkling
Salt, 2 pinches

Place apples on a greased cookie sheet, cover with nonstick spray, and sprinkle with spices. Bake at 450°F for 15 minutes, or until soft.


## BANANA ICE CREAM (DAIRY)

2 large frozen bananas, cut up
1 C. milk or plain yogurt

1/2 tsp. vanilla extract*

Peel and cut bananas before freezing. Remove frozen bananas from freezer and allow to thaw for two minutes. Put bananas in a blender with milk or yogurt and vanilla extract.
* Vanilla extract is a sweetener and should not be used by those who are abstaining from sweeteners.

96

# SORBET

2 lbs. frozen fruit (mango,          1 can frozen apple juice
strawberries, blueberries, or        concentrate*
cherries)

Do not thaw either the fruit or the apple juice concentrate. Puree fruit
and apple juice concentrate in a food processor using the S-blade.
Freeze. Take out of the freezer about half hour before serving. Serve a
small scoop of different flavors in the same bowl for a very colorful and
elegant presentation.
* Apple juice concentrate is a sweetener and should not be used by
those who are abstaining from sweeteners.

# BANANA SPICE CAKE

1 C. oat bran                        6 oz. unsweetened applesauce
3 eggs                               1/2 tsp. cinnamon
3/4 tsp. baking soda                 1/2 tsp. cardamom
3 very ripe bananas, sliced or 16    1 tsp. vanilla extract
    oz. baby food bananas

Beat all ingredients with mixer. Pour into greased loaf pan. Bake at
350°F for about 30 minutes.

# APPLE CAKE

Top and bottom cake layers:          1/2 C. orange juice
3 C. oatmeal or oat bran             Apple Filling:
1 jar banana baby food               6 apples, grated
3/4 C. oil                           1/2 tsp. cinnamon
4 eggs                               1 tsp. vanilla extract*
1 1/4 tsp. baking powder

Mix the cake ingredients together well. Prepare apple filling in a
separate bowl. Place half of the oat mixture in a greased baking pan.
Pour the apple filling on next, and then top with the other half of the oat
mixture. Bake at 350°F for 1 hour.
* Vanilla extract is a sweetener and should not be used by those who
are abstaining from sweeteners.

# AMBROSIA

1 can pineapple chunks, drained
2 C. unsweetened coconut
  flakes
3 bananas, sliced

3 oranges, diced
1 C. toasted pecans, chopped
1 tsp. cinnamon
1 tsp. nutmeg

Mix ingredients and chill.


# COCONUT BALLS

1/2 C. raisins
3/4 C. walnuts
1/2 C. dried dates, pitted
1/2 C. dried apricots

2 T. orange juice
1 tsp. zest of of one orange
1 small bag unsweetened
  shredded coconut

In a food processor, process raisins, walnuts, dates and apricots for
1-2 minutes or until finely chopped. Add juice and zest and blend for
1-2 minutes more. Chill mixture in refrigerator for 15 minutes. Dampen
hands, form mixture into balls, and roll them in coconut. Store balls in
refrigerator.


# CRUNCHY PEANUT BUTTER BALLS

1 C. unsweetened puffed rice
  cereal, mashed

3/4 C. unsweetened peanut or
  soy nut butter

Mix very well. Form into balls and freeze.


# JUICY "SODA"

Unflavored seltzer

100% orange or grape juice

Mix about 2/3 seltzer to 1/3 juice. Serve instead of soda.
Variation: Add a scoop of sorbet to seltzer and juice for an ice cream
float.

## BANANA SMOOTHIE (DAIRY OR PAREVE)

2 large bananas
1 C. milk or unsweetened soy
  milk
1/2 C. orange juice

1/2 C. ground almonds or 2 T.
  unsweetened peanut butter
Dash of cinnamon

Put all the ingredients in a blender and blend until smooth.

## MELON SMOOTHIE

1 C. chopped melon (any kind)
2 pears, peeled and chopped

1 C. grape juice
2 ice cubes

Put all the ingredients in a blender and blend until smooth.

## PINA COLADA (PAREVE OR DAIRY)

1 C. milk or unsweetened soy
  milk
1 C. pineapple, chopped

1 tsp. coconut extract
5 ice cubes

Combine all ingredients in blender and blend until creamy.

## BLUEBERRY SHAKE (DAIRY)

1 1/2 C. frozen blueberries
1/2 C. plain yogurt

1 C. apple juice

Combine ingredients in a blender until smooth.

## SENSATIONAL STRAWBERRY SMOOTHIE (DAIRY OR PAREVE)

1 C. frozen strawberries
2 bananas

1 C. milk or grape juice or
  orange juice

Place all ingredients in blender and blend.

## ALMOND SMOOTHIE (DAIRY OR PAREVE)

1 1/2 C. cold unsweetened soy
   milk or milk
1 T. almond butter
2 drops vanilla extract*

5 dates
2 T. raisins
1 T. carob powder
5 ice cubes

Blend almond butter and milk to make a nice thick creamy shake. Add dates, raisins, vanilla, carob powder, and ice.
* Vanilla extract is a sweetener and should not be used by those who are abstaining from sweeteners.

## MELON MANGO SMOOTHIE (DAIRY)

1/2 cantaloupe, cubed
1/2 mango, cubed

1 C. plain yogurt
5 ice cubes

Combine ingredients in blender until smooth.

## TOFU SMOOTHIE

1 1/2 C. frozen strawberries
1 banana

1/2 C. soft tofu

In a food processor or blender, process all the ingredients until smooth. Add a little chilled water for thinner smoothies if desired.

## CREAMY DREAMY NUTTY AVOCADO SHAKE (DAIRY)

1 banana
1/2 ripe avocado
1/2 ripe peach
2 T. roasted unsalted pumpkin
   seeds, optional
2 T. walnut pieces

1/2 C. unsweetened almond milk
1/2 C. plain yogurt
1/4 C. cottage cheese
Water, as needed

Place all ingredients in a blender and blend until smooth. Add enough water until consistency is to your liking. Serves 2.

# Single Serving Dishes

## HEARTY FRUIT BREAKFAST LOAF (DAIRY)

2 oz. Old-Fashioned oats or oat bran
1 egg
4 oz. milk

6 oz. fruit (apple, blueberry, peach, pineapple, or banana work well)
Cinnamon or pumpkin pie spice

Mix all the ingredients together. Bake at 350°F in a greased mini loaf pan for 45 minutes. This keeps well in the refrigerator or freezer. Option: For quicker cooking, can be cooked in a frying pan as a pancake.

## BLUEBERRY OAT BRAN PANCAKES

6 oz. blueberries (either fresh or frozen)

2 oz. oat bran
2 eggs

Mix ingredients. Heat a skillet or griddle over medium heat. Cook the first side for 2 minutes or until the bubbles that form on the top pop. Flip it over and let the other side cook for about a minute or until golden brown.

## BREAKFAST BAR (DAIRY)

2 oz. ricotta cheese
2 oz. farmer cheese
6 oz. crushed pineapple, drained

2 oz. Old-Fashioned oats or oat bran
Lemon juice to taste

Combine ingredients. Bake in greased baking pan at 350°F for approximately 25 minutes.

## BREAKFAST SOUFFLÉ

4 egg whites, slightly beaten
2 oz. Old-Fashioned oats

6 oz. applesauce

Spray microwave-safe bowl with nonstick spray. Place all ingredients in bowl, mix well and microwave covered for 2 minutes.

101

# CHEESECAKE

3 oz. cottage cheese           6 oz. crushed pineapple, drained
1 egg white

Beat ingredients together. Pour into a greased loaf pan and bake at 350°F for 45 minutes.

## EGGPLANT PARMESAN (DAIRY)

6 oz. eggplant                 1/2 oz. butter
2 oz. tomato sauce             4 oz. brown rice, cooked
2 oz. shredded cheese

Peel and slice eggplant. Place sliced eggplant in a colander and sprinkle salt over eggplant and let stand 10 minutes; rinse salt and pat dry. Place eggplant on greased cookie sheet, and bake at 350°F for 30 minutes or sauté eggplant for 10 minutes.
Once eggplant is baked, place cooked brown rice in bottom of small, greased baking pan, then place eggplant, tomato sauce, and shredded cheese on top in layers. Bake uncovered at 400°F for a few minutes until cheese melts and browns slightly.

## BROCCOLI QUICHE

Frozen chopped broccoli,       1 egg, beaten
    thawed and drained         1 oz. shredded mozzarella
1 small onion, finely diced        cheese
1 clove garlic, minced         1/2 tsp. black pepper
1 tsp. salt                    1 T. butter

Spray a non-stick pan and sauté broccoli, onion, and garlic 10 - 15 minutes. Weigh cooked vegetables to appropriate amount for your food plan. Combine vegetables with egg, salt, pepper, and butter. Pour vegetable mixture into greased baking pan, top with shredded cheese. Bake at 350°F for 30 minutes.

## VEGETABLE LASAGNA (DAIRY)

8 oz. cooked zucchini, onion, eggplant, peppers, tomato sauce

2 oz. ricotta cheese

1 oz. shredded mozzarella cheese

4 oz. cooked brown rice

Cook the vegetables in a pot or in the microwave. Weigh vegetables and add cooked brown rice and ricotta cheese. Mix. Pour mixture into a small, greased baking pan. Sprinkle mozzarella cheese on top and bake at 400°F for a few minutes until cheese melts.

## VEGETABLE LUNCH LOAF

16 oz. shredded zucchini, carrots, and onion, sautéed

2 eggs

2 oz. raw oats or oat bran

1 T. oil

1/4 tsp. curry

1/4 tsp. salt

Sauté onion until golden. Add zucchini and carrots. In a separate bowl, mix eggs, oats, and oil together. Weigh vegetables and mix with oat mixture and spices. Spray a loaf pan, and pour in mixture. Bake 45 minutes at 350°F.

## QUICK & EASY MEAL

8 oz. frozen or canned vegetables

4 oz. brown rice, cooked

2 eggs

1 T. margarine or butter

2-3 tsp. Bragg's liquid aminos (or soy sauce)

Sauté vegetables and rice. Beat eggs and add them to the pan. Cook as a scrambled egg mixture. Sprinkle with the soy sauce.
Variation 1: Instead of eggs, use tofu or canned beans.
Variation 2: Instead of soy sauce, use curry.

# BARLEY SALAD

4 oz. barley, cooked
4 oz. garbanzo beans
16 oz. cucumbers and peppers, chopped

1/2 oz. olive oil
Salt and pepper

Place 1 C. barley in 3 C. boiling water, lower heat, cover, and simmer until water is absorbed. Weigh out appropriate amount of barley for your food plan. Add remaining ingredients and mix.

## GRILLED CHICKEN AVOCADO SALAD

4 oz. grilled chicken, cubed
2 oz. avocado, cubed
2 oz. canned corn
2 oz. hearts of palm, sliced
2 oz. grape tomatoes, sliced in half

1 T. mayonnaise
1/8 tsp. salt
1 tsp. dill
Lemon juice

Soak avocado in lemon juice. Mix all ingredients (except avocado) together. Drain avocado and lightly toss into salad.

## EASY SALMON PATTIES

3 oz. canned skinless, boneless salmon
1 egg white, beaten
2 oz. oat bran

1 tsp. lemon juice
1 tsp. salt
1/4 tsp. dill
1 tsp. onion flakes

Drain the liquid from the can of salmon into a bowl and mix the liquid with egg white, lemon juice, spices and oat bran. Mix in salmon. Add a bit of water if needed so that the mixture is moist. Spray a frying pan with nonstick cooking spray. Form mixture into patties and fry for 5 minutes on each side. Serve with mayonnaise and vegetable slices.

# GREEK SALAD

8 oz. lettuce, peppers, tomatoes,          1 T. olive oil
   red onion, black olives               Lemon juice
4 oz. feta cheese

Chop and combine vegetables. Grate feta cheese with grater or crumble with hands. Mix olive oil and lemon juice and pour over salad.

# POTATO BLINTZES

Blintz:                                    Filling:
2 eggs, beaten                             2 potatoes, peeled and cubed
1/4 tsp. salt                              1/4 tsp. salt
1/4 C. water                               Onion flakes
                                           Garlic Powder
                                           Black Pepper

Beat the eggs, water and salt together. Heat a greased small pan over medium heat until hot. Place 2 tablespoons of egg mixture into pan. Cook until the bottom is browned. Carefully flip over and cook about one more minute. Slide blintz onto a plate. Continue making blintzes until egg mixture is gone.

Cook cubed potatoes in salt water. When soft, mash and add spices. Place potato mixture (use a liberal amount but not too much so that it doesn't spill out of the blintz) about a quarter of the way in on one side of the blintz. Roll the crepe over the filling, keeping it tight. Your filling will fall out if you've rolled the blintz loosely. Place the filled blintz seam side down on the plate so it doesn't open.

# SPAGHETTI SQUASH COLESLAW

1 spaghetti squash                         1 T. mayonnaise
carrots, shredded                          1 tsp. white vinegar
Pickles, diced

Pierce squash in several places with knife or fork. Cook whole squash for about 10 minutes in microwave, until tender. Alternatively, you can slice the squash in half, place face down in a baking pan and bake for 30- 40 minutes at 375°F
Weigh out 8 oz. of spaghetti squash, carrots, and pickles and mix. Mix with mayonnaise and vinegar.

# FRUIT SORBET

6 oz. fresh fruit (combination of
   any - e.g. mango, blueberries,
   strawberries, cherries, peaches,
   pineapple, or bananas)

Puree fruit in blender and freeze.
Dairy variation, blend fruit with 8 oz. plain yogurt and freeze.

# OAT ROLLS

| | |
|---|---|
| 12 oz. 1-minute quick oats | 1 1/2 tsp. salt |
| 2 C. water | 2 T. onion flakes, optional |

Mix ingredients well. The dough will be sticky. Let dough sit for 1/2 hour to thicken. With wet hands, form into 6 balls. Place balls on a greased pan and bake for 30 minutes at 350°F. Serve warm. These can be used on Shabbos instead of challah for people who are allergic to flour.

# CROSS REFERENCE INDEX

b

d

## CHEESE DISHES

## CHICKEN

f

h

j

k

I

m

## PARSNIPS

## PEAS

## PEPPERS

r

## TOFU

## TOMATO

U